Having been in ministry for many years, educated at Wheaton, Trinity, and McCormack, I have been exposed to quality teaching. Jerry Miller's new book, *Grace Beyond Reason*, is the best book on God's grace I have ever read. I consider it to be a book of great spiritual depth. Jerry gives us an amazingly accurate theology of grace, focusing on the nature of grace as empowerment, as well as grace in relation to the law and commandments of God. It is so very trustworthy in theology. However, I could not just read it for theology alone. Once I got into the book, I realized the quality of the content for personal growth and had to read it devotionally. I believe I grew through reading the book in this way. I cannot over emphasize the importance of *Grace Beyond Reason*. It has transformative power. As you take the time to go through it and absorb its content, you will be changed and will approach your life in God with much greater success and joy.

Dr. Daniel C. Juster, Th.D.
Restoration from Zion, Tikkun Global, Jerusalem

Reading through Jerry Miller's new book, *Grace Beyond Reason*, one will lay hold of truth after truth. This book is so needed at the present time, as we navigate between the prevailing thoughts and teachings of the Grace movement. I appreciate how Jerry highlights the difference between Grace and Mercy, showing how grace is more than unmerited favor, but rather, the empowerment for living the life as a follower of Messiah. He effectively navigates between the opposite extremes of "easy" grace as well as unreachable grace. The "faithful and just" section, towards the end of chapter four is not only sound but is material to be meditated on. To sum it up, Jerry Miller's teaching on grace is a MUST READ! But from his own words toward the end of the last chapter, "grace must become revelation to us so we will not be slaves to our mind's struggle to receive grace." Thank you, Jerry, for this timely gem!

Michael Modica
Pastor, First Assembly, Deland, FL
Presbyter, Peninsular Florida District, Police Chaplain

Jerry Miller is a solid, grounded, mature teacher of the Word, and in this inspiring book, he opens up the treasures of God's marvelous grace. The grace of God brings peace, hope, joy, and the power to become more like the Messiah. The grace of God liberates! Whether you struggle with feelings of regret and never measuring up, whether you live under a cloud of condemnation, or whether you simply want to be immersed all over again in what the Scriptures say about God's grace, you will be blessed and encouraged by this book.

Dr. Michael L. Brown
Host, Line of Fire broadcast
President of Fire School of Ministry

Jerry Miller has been a dear friend and partner in ministry for over forty years! His roots in the Messianic movement go back to the 1970s. Jerry is an excellent systematic student and teacher of Scriptures, whose presentations are line by line, very ordered and logically laid out. His messages are always faith building and uplifting, leaving those who hear him encouraged. I hope, as you read the chapters in this book, you will be able to sense some of the special qualities that mark Jerry's life and ministry.

Asher Intrater
Revive Israel, Tikkun Global, Jerusalem

I believe *Grace Beyond Reason* will lead to much growth and breakthrough. Those who read it will experience a renewing of their minds, transforming how they see God, themselves and others. Part of this personal renewing is in the area of intimate worship and prayer. It will certainly aid in the life transformation we all need, as we are in process of becoming more like Yeshua. I believe the book will even help to save marriages. I do not doubt that this book will have a special impact on leaders, changing how we live and lead as kingdom sons and daughters, led by the Spirit.

Richard Cleary
Kingdom Living Messianic Congregation, Shawnee, KS

This book is a *mekor chochma* (Hebrew for fountain of wisdom) for all who want to experience more of the grace of God in their lives—every day and throughout the day. It is encouraging and practical. I highly recommend it!

Dr. David J. Rudolph, Ph.D.
Director of Messianic Jewish Studies, The King's University

Jerry Miller tells the truth. Whatever he's talking about, teaching on, or privately sharing, I believe him. This trust comes from a treasured friendship and shared ministry that go back nearly forty years. In this valuable book, *Grace Beyond Reason,* he explores the anatomy of God's amazing, unreasonable grace. Could there be a more important subject? I think not. So—read on and be taken up into a fresh measure of who God made you to be!

Eitan Shishkoff
Founding Director, Tents of Mercy Network,
Kiryat Yam, Israel

Rabbi Jerry Miller has lived, walked out, and exhorted us in God's grace for over forty years! I have sat under his teaching and served alongside him, and the content of *Grace Beyond Reason* is not just an exercise in theological rhetoric. While he gives us an exhaustive understanding of God's unreasonable grace, there is more to this book than knowledge alone. What is in its pages is the experiential and life-changing power of Grace. Jerry shares of a reality that he has both received and lived, and into which he has discipled others. This book is for any and all who are looking to receive and walk in Yeshua's Grace more fully.

Todd R. Westphal
Senior leader, El Shaddai Congregation, Frederick, MD

Jerry Miller's book on grace is the best book I have read on this topic. I was brought to tears reading the opening chapters, as the words and message ministered to me deeply. Reading this book opened the eyes of my heart to an even greater understanding of grace, imparting a faith for entering into new levels of God's grace in my own walk. I have read most of the book twice, and my first time through, I did not want the book to come to an end…just like a good meal. The book has transformative power in teaching us how to overcome condemnation, and how to enter into an inexpressible joy and peace beyond understanding. This book is so needed today, especially in light of the challenges of our day. I can think of so many people I would like to send a copy to, and even now, I have begun using it in mentoring other women, who have shared of its impact on their lives. I highly recommend this book, for new believers, or even the most seasoned followers of Yeshua. All will be blessed from reading *Grace Beyond Reason*.

Patricia Juster
Restoration from Zion, Jerusalem

Without the biblical understanding of grace, you will NEVER enter into the fullness of the Kingdom of God in this life. Without the full biblical knowledge of grace, you will never operate in the supernatural and be "normal." That is, normal according to the pattern of the Bible!

Sid Roth
Host, "It's Supernatural"

Amazing Grace, how sweet the sound! What a treasure this

book is. With overwhelming love and gratitude, I recommend this great work, *Grace Beyond Reason*. This book is truly a gift. Jerry has spent decades peering into the wonder of God's grace, and what he has found, and shares with us in this book, proves it was worth every moment. Thank you, Jerry, for bringing us into what you have seen. It is glorious! May God's grace abound all the more.

Leah Ramirez
Founder, Ask for the Nations

The inner self has always been a primary interest for Jerry Miller. His long term, deeply pondered thought and study have really come out in his book, *Grace Beyond Reason*. In reading this book, I feel I have been exposed to a revelatory understanding of grace, seeing grace more fully as a dynamic feature of our spiritual growth. Dig deep into this well-written, easy read.

Paul Liberman
Messianic Rabbi, Palm Springs, CA

In Rabbi Jerry Miller's book, *Grace Beyond Reason*, we find laced throughout these pages of profound truth, his own personal journey of childlike faith, revealed in transparent humility. The very candor of his unveiled heart impels us into the kind of intimate conversation often only whispered between closest of lifelong friends. This book is a gripping trove of priceless pearls strung together brilliantly. I'm hoping we might soon see a *Grace Beyond Reason* Study Guide as a companion to the book.

David C. Rudolph
Founder, Gateways Beyond International

As part of the millennial generation, I have seen extreme doctrines and teaching on the subject of grace. *Grace Beyond Reason* brings a scripture-based, Spirit-led, faith-filled approach with clarity. This is so helpful, because the concept of grace can often seem intangible. Rabbi Jerry Miller brings practical application and relevancy to receiving and experiencing the grace of the Lord in your everyday life. He brings balance to understanding and living a life overflowing in the inheritance of grace from God. The message of this book is vital for all believers and transcends generational boundaries. *Grace Beyond Reason* is a beautiful resource for your personal devotional life and is an excellent discipleship training and equipping tool for ministry leaders. As you read this book, you will experience the supernatural gift of grace being opened up and released into your life.

Andrew Gudgeon
Executive Pastor
El Shaddai Congregation

Jerry Miller is a seasoned pastor, teacher and Messianic theologian. His maturity is demonstrated in this book, *Grace Beyond Reason*. In a day of extremes, Jerry finds the dynamic tension of truth in a balanced way yet without compromise. This book is a must-read for new believers as well as seasoned saints.

Terry King
Alliance International Ministries

GRACE
BEYOND
REASON

THE UNTAPPED SECRET
TO THE LIFE GOD INTENDS

JERRY MILLER

HIGHERLIFE
PUBLISHING & MARKETING

Grace Beyond Reason

Published by HigherLife Development Services Inc.
PO Box 623307
Oviedo, Florida 32762
www.ahigherlife.com

Copyright © 2021 Jerry A. Miller

ISBN: 978-1-954533-09-7 (Paperback)
978-1-954533-10-3 (ebook)
Library of Congress Control Number: 2021903025

Printed in the United States of America.

10 9 8 7 6 5 4 3 2 1
Printed in the United States of America

DEDICATION

I dedicate this book to our glorious God, who amazes me daily as He displays, in so many ways, His love, goodness, majesty, and power. Thank You, Lord, for opening my eyes and my heart to who You are and for giving so much to one so undeserving. May I never grow weary of learning and growing in Your unreasonable grace.

I also dedicate this book to my wife, Jo, the love of my life, my best friend, and my life partner. For forty-four years, you have been my greatest encourager, always challenging me to see what God Himself sees in me and to not settle for less. You are God's gift to my life. I love you and thank God for you!

Finally, I dedicate this book to my children, grandchildren, and all the younger generations. May God's unreasonable grace equip and prepare you to "take the torch" and run your race for His glory! May your hearts always be gripped with a consuming passion for fulfilling your destiny to prepare the way for Messiah's return.

ACKNOWLEDGMENTS

In addition to those involved with this book specifically, I want to acknowledge and thank a few who have had broader impact on my life as a follower of Yeshua.

To Frank and Carolyn Taylor, who took me under their wing when I first came to faith in Jesus. Thank you for your patience in answering my multitude of questions, as we sat in your living room week after week. Thank you for your role in discipling me, as well as in reintroducing me to my Jewish heritage.

To Daniel Juster and David C. Rudolph. For decades, you have been spiritual fathers to me, displaying Yeshua through teaching, mentoring, and friendship. You have sown immeasurably into my life, modeling zeal for God and His Kingdom, as well as love for people.

To those I have enjoyed the privilege of co-laboring with over the years. I have been truly privileged to walk in covenant friendship and partnership with so many amazing people, too many to name individually. Your zeal for God, and passionate pursuit of Him, has continually stirred and inspired me, leaving me unwilling to settle for anything less for my own life.

To the intercessors and prayer warriors who have lifted us up over the years. Although you have labored "behind the scenes," seen only by God, your prayers have been key to the outworking of God's grace in our lives. Thank you for your faithful obedience!

To Todd Westphal, who first suggested, more than twenty years ago, that I needed to write books. Thank you for bringing it up year after year. You have been a consistent source of encouragement in this, especially as this book began to take shape.

To my wife, Jo, who was my "sounding board" and proof-reader as each chapter was being written. I could not have finished this without your constant help and encouragement.

To Grant Berry, who connected me to HigherLife Publishing. To HigherLife's president, David Welday, who saw value in this book and believed it needed to be published.

To Andrew Ste. Marie of HigherLife, who has walked me through the process of publishing my first book, patiently answering my ongoing questions. To Libbye Morris, for her excellent work of editing.

CONTENTS

FOREWORD

I t brings me much joy to write the foreword for this book. Actually, it's about more than just a book. Full disclosure: Jerry Miller has been a close personal friend of mine for nearly four decades. Two of our children were born during the same season in the same hospital; our wives worked and worshiped alongside us at Beth Messiah Congregation in Rockville, Maryland; and Jerry and I served as elders and leaders with Sid Roth, Dr. Daniel Juster, Dr. Michael Brown, and others. We served together for the entire decade of the 1980s. In short, we are covenant friends for life, and beyond. While our leadership team included several well-schooled and credentialed teachers, Jerry was often called on to teach, preach, lead home groups, and serve as an elder and associate minister.

In *Grace Beyond Reason*, Jerry deals with many aspects of grace that may not be obvious to the casual observer. He begins with the distinction between grace and mercy, going beyond the oversimplified definitions commonly heard. He delves deeply into the subject matter early on, making it clear that the grace of God is actually more amazing than we realize. In my opinion, this book is well worth your time and attention, if only for those pages alone. But don't speed-read or skim through the introduction quickly, or else you will miss the premise for the entire book.

Pay particular attention to the number of times Jerry speaks about grace as God's provision for bringing an empowerment to do something. More than the power of God to forgive, the grace that Jerry speaks about here has the power to change the one who receives this grace. For this reason, I don't believe I would be far off the mark by saying that, according to what Jerry shares with us, grace goes well beyond God's favor in forgiving sin, as it is about His power given to us to overcome sin, and more. This, in my mind, is a huge distinction for us as followers of Yeshua (Jesus). Realizing this should motivate us to cry out daily for a fuller understanding and experience of this grace that causes us to triumph over sin, rather than asking only for the grace of His forgiveness every time we miss the mark!

In chapter after chapter, Jerry uncovers different aspects of the far-reaching nature of grace, but he never falls into the theological trap of what some might call "hyper-grace." The grace of God is truly amazing, as the hymn writer so beautifully portrayed many years ago. My belief and expectation is that you will be amazed again and again as you consider the words and concepts presented here in *Grace Beyond Reason*.

Paul Wilbur
Worship Artist/Pastor
Wilbur Ministries

INTRODUCTION

I n some respects, the early years of my personal journey did not exactly *prepare* me to write a book on God's *grace*. Don't get me wrong—I desperately *needed* grace, but I surely did not know it for many years. The truth is, I had no idea what grace even was. I grew up in a nonreligious Jewish family, and the idea of grace simply had no relevance to me. I thought grace was a prayer that Christians prayed before eating their meals, and nothing more.

But everything changed when, at age twenty-five, I became convinced that Yeshua (Hebrew for *Jesus*) truly is the Messiah, and I committed my life to Him. While the *work* of God's grace was dramatic in bringing change to my life, my *comprehension* of grace was a work in progress. I learned the importance of grace as a basic doctrine, and that grace, rather than good works, is to be the basis for our relationship with God. But honestly, grace was more of a mere *concept* to me than a life-giving, dynamic truth. In spite of my limited understanding, my salvation experience truly was radical in the sense that I gave myself wholeheartedly to the Lord and grew very quickly in my faith. My life changed significantly, and that alone speaks to me of the amazing nature of God and His grace. God is so

> *God is so committed to our transformation that He will do a powerful work of grace in us, even as we lack understanding of that grace.*

committed to our transformation that He will do a powerful *work* of grace in us, even as we lack *understanding* of that grace.

But I *do* believe it is God's desire that we *discover* grace as a life-giving truth that is to have a dynamic impact on us throughout our lives. Such discovery results in our *experiencing* grace far beyond a mere knowledge of grace as a doctrine or idea. Such discovery, energized by our growing faith and the presence and work of the Holy Spirit in our lives, is to be a catalyst for a life in which God takes us beyond our natural limitations.

I recall quite clearly the season of my life when "the light went on," so to speak, and I began to see with greater clarity the awesome nature of the grace of God. The Lord had put in my heart a desire to memorize portions of Scripture. At that time, I focused on Paul's letter to the congregation in Rome, and I memorized chapters four through eight. I would regularly go jogging and take index cards with me, going over sections of the chapters at a time as I ran. The process went on for months, resulting in significant time meditating on the passages. These chapters "came alive" in me in a whole new way, giving me fresh and powerful insight into God's grace and our life in Yeshua as Paul was teaching it.

Far beyond intellectual knowledge, I felt God was giving me revelation into these areas. The result was life changing for me personally. My concept of God, my concept of myself, as well as of others, and my concept of my calling and destiny were all impacted. My eyes were being opened to see the magnitude of God's grace and His intended impact of grace in our lives. Every time I felt God giving me fresh insight, my heart was stirred with an excitement for teaching it. Grace became a "life message" for me as I sought to make it central in most of the messages that I shared in our congregation.

LIFE IN THE "IMPOSSIBLE" REALM

Our walk of faith in Yeshua involves so many different areas that are clearly beyond our natural ability. Considering these areas can leave us wondering how we can possibly live the life to which God calls us. We ask ourselves questions like this:

- How can I live in freedom from condemnation and shame when I know how miserably I have let God down?
- How can I walk in holiness and purity when I am bombarded with temptation, and my flesh so often wants to go its own way?
- How can I embrace the life of sacrifice, giving, and serving when I so often feel the pull of self-centeredness?
- How can I love the unlovable?
- How can I forgive and be gracious when people offend me?
- How can I be confident in *God's* love after experiencing so much rejection from *people?*
- How can I stand strong if I experience suffering for my faith?
- How can I actually *represent God* to a hostile and unbelieving world?

> *For every aspect of life and calling that appears impossible to us, grace is God's answer and provision.*

God's *grace* is the answer to each of these questions and so many more like them. God's grace brings a supernatural influence and equips us to live beyond the limits of our natural capabilities. For every aspect of life and calling that appears impossible to us, grace is God's answer and provision.

Every blessing of salvation is experienced through the working of God's grace. When we limit grace to the simple idea of unmerited favor and mercy, as it is so often defined, we minimize the meaning and the goal of grace. We must gain a fuller and clearer vision for what grace accomplishes in us. *Every* follower of Yeshua needs God's grace. It is not just for the so-called "weak"—even the most seasoned and mature believer will never outgrow the need for grace.

Yet there is a difficulty we all face. We can be familiar with grace as a *doctrine* or *concept* while still finding it challenging to *receive* and *live* in grace. Many potential hindrances are at work to prevent us from *walking* in that which we know in our *minds*. Again, this is why we must come into a heart revelation of grace. We need this revelation because grace is too big to fit into the limitations of our natural reasoning. It goes far beyond what the mind can comprehend. It is *beyond reason*, which is one reason why grace is truly so *amazing*, as the well-known song declares. The very quality that makes grace amazing is also what can make it so challenging for us to walk in. Thus, we must learn to recognize and deal with those practical challenges that can keep us from the fullness of life into which grace brings us.

SEEING OUR GLORIOUS CALLING

Every follower of Yeshua has a glorious calling that is beyond comprehension. This includes *unique* assignments God has for us as individuals. It also includes the *universal* calling and destiny for *every* believer to be conformed into Yeshua's likeness and to represent Him to a world that is lost and needs to know Him. God's grace is key to unlocking this calling and empowering us to walk it out. No wonder the enemy of our souls has sought to bring such confusion about the grace of God! Confusion abounds, both in *defining* grace as well as *applying* it. Today, a *false* grace message is being taught in some circles.

Believers are being misled to think that grace "frees" us from having to be accountable to God's standards and instruction. Many believe that God does not *require* anything of us in terms of obedience and how we live. Crucial issues such as the fear of the Lord, conviction of sin, confession of sin, and repentance are downplayed, and seen as irrelevant to the believer who is now "under grace." Such thinking is deception, misrepresenting the *nature and goal* of grace. It can lead folks to think that grace provides us with an excuse or a cover for disobedience or rebellion.

But nothing could be further from the truth. As we learn of God's grace and grow in our revelation of it we will be led to *embrace* God's highest ways for our lives. Grace does not *relieve* us of the responsibility to aim for high standards. Grace is what takes away our *excuses* for *settling* in compromise. To use slightly different wording, grace does not provide us with a *way out* from obedience and holiness. Instead, grace gives us a pathway *into* a life in which holiness becomes truly possible. You see, grace *empowers* us for the walk of holiness to which God's Word calls us. Grace empowers us for a life that *demonstrates* our loyalty and allegiance to the One who has saved us and given us eternal life.

WHY WRITE ANOTHER BOOK ON GRACE?

In preparing to write this book, I found myself asking the question (probably dozens of times) of whether the body of Messiah really needs *another* book on grace. After all, so much has already been written and powerfully communicated on this topic. The truth is, we can *know about* grace while still experiencing challenges in actually *appropriating* grace in our lives.

> *Grace does not relieve us of the responsibility to aim for high standards. Grace is what takes away our excuses for settling in compromise.*

So in writing this book my intent is not to provide an exhaustive study on grace. Rather, my hope is to encourage a fresh inspiration, and hopefully revelation, related to the magnificence of what grace can accomplish in our lives. My desire is that grace would come alive for you in a fresh way, giving you *practical* insight into the nature of grace. In this regard, I have focused on both challenges as well as help for *receiving* grace and *walking* in it. God's grace must become practical to us, not just an idea with minimal impact. My hope is that, in sharing my own experiences and challenges in appropriating grace, you might be encouraged in your walk to enter God's amazing grace more fully.

CHAPTER ONE

ACCESS BY FAITH

*"Therefore, having been made righteous by trusting, we
have shalom with God through our Lord Yeshua the
Messiah. Through Him we also have gained access by faith
into this grace in which we stand..."*
—ROMANS 5:1–2

I n Paul's letter to the believers in Rome, he makes a statement that is foundational to the life into which God calls
us as followers of Yeshua (Jesus). At the core of our spiritual
lives is the principle of faith, or *trusting* in the perfect righteousness of Yeshua as the basis for our own relationship with
God. Rather than leaning on our own righteous acts, we put
our trust in the righteousness of another—the sinless Messiah
and son of God. Trusting in Him and not ourselves, we are
forgiven by God, and we receive Yeshua's perfect righteousness. Our sin, which resulted in a barrier between God and
ourselves, is taken away, and we come into a relational peace
with God. This is basic "Theology101." We are reconciled with
God and made righteous by faith.

MERCY IS DIFFERENT FROM GRACE

But Paul is saying so much more here, and the key is in verse 2. There we read that faith is also the basis for access *into* grace. Verse 1 highlights God's *mercy* in forgiving us and making peace with us. This is *one aspect* of God's grace, but our forgiveness is just the beginning of a *life* lived in the realm of God's grace. Too often, we wrongly see *mercy* and *grace* as simply two different words for the same thing. Actually, they are different because they describe different aspects of God's work in us.

Mercy relates to our sins and failures. Because God is merciful, He forgives us as we trust in Yeshua's death and resurrection. *Grace* is broader in scope, impacting our personal transformation as well as empowerment for a life that honors God as we represent Him to others. *Mercy* relates to our past and present sins, offering us freedom from the guilt of our past and present. *Grace* relates to our present and future calling and destiny, offering us empowerment for a supernatural life once we receive forgiveness. *Mercy* releases us from the debt we owe, freeing us from the judgment we deserve. *Grace* empowers us for a life in which God wants to take us beyond our natural abilities.

> *Mercy is a gateway into a life in which God's grace brings supernatural empowerment to us.*

I am not suggesting there is no overlap between mercy and grace. Yes, God's mercy to us is clearly an *aspect* of His grace. But forgiveness is just a beginning point for an entire *life* marked by grace. We might say that mercy is a gateway into a life in which God's grace brings supernatural empowerment to us. God's *mercy* is that He forgives us and brings us into relationship with Himself, even though we are undeserving. God's *grace* is that He equips and empowers us for a holy and transformed life and calling. God's mercy is indeed a glorious gift to us, but it is just the beginning of a grace-filled adventure with God, in which we experience transformation and empowerment beyond natural ability or comprehension.

Coming back to Paul's point in Romans 5, faith is what opens the way to be forgiven and reconciled to God. Faith is also what gives us access into the supernatural realm of grace. Let me offer a simple summary description. *Grace* is the undeserved, yet freely given, gift from God to man, enabling man to be forgiven and brought into *relationship* with God, for growing into the *calling and assignment* God has for every individual.

Paul himself provides us with a powerful example of this truth. In his first letter to the believers in Corinth he explains that, based on his past sins, he was not worthy to be called an emissary, or apostle (1 Cor. 15:9). But he goes on to say, "by the grace of God I am what I am. His grace toward me was not in vain…" (1 Cor. 15:10). God's grace blesses us beyond what we deserve and empowers us for a calling beyond what is reasonable. Thus, God essentially "forces" us to function in the realm of *faith* because that is the only way of *access into* His grace. Our failures and past sins do not disqualify us. The only thing that keeps us from entering relationship with, and destiny in, God is our *unwillingness* to enter His grace, as we focus instead on our shortcomings.

While grace does include God's mercy and undeserved favor, it is not limited to that. Grace is about divine empowerment for life and godliness, bringing transformation to our own lives and a testimony of Yeshua to those around us. I don't claim this to be the ultimate definition of grace, but it does provide a framework for the focus of this book.

THE NEED FOR REVELATION

Once we come to faith in Yeshua as Messiah and commit to a life of allegiance to Him as Lord, the revelation of God's *grace* is the most impacting revelation we can ever take hold of as followers of Yeshua. We see in the New Covenant Scriptures that God Himself has a goal for our lives. First, God seeks *relationship*. In response to God's love for us, we are called to *love Him* with all our "heart…soul and…strength" (Deut. 6:5). Then we are "to be conformed to the image of His Son" (Rom. 8:29).

This is truly a stunning concept to consider. As we walk in loving relationship with the Lord, we as believers are being *transformed* by the work of God's Spirit in our lives. The result of this transforming work is that we are to experience and display a growing resemblance to Yeshua Himself. How can we even conceive of such a thing? Well, the truth is, our finite minds *cannot* conceive of it, and that is why we do need *revelation* in this area. Such a destiny is far beyond anything we could figure out with our minds. Thus, only revelation by God's Spirit can enable us to see this and believe it is possible.

God invites each of us into this realm of His grace, a realm in which the impossible becomes possible.

Revelation enables us to see and embrace, by faith, this lofty goal God sets before us. And then, God's *grace* brings the empowerment for us to actually come into the fulfillment of the goal over the course of our lives. We can never grow into Yeshua's likeness, or represent Him to those around us, through the striving of our human efforts alone. It is a work of God's grace. We cannot take any credit for it, yet we do have a part to play. Human effort is involved, as God does not just do a supernatural work in us while we remain passive. What is our part? We must pursue Him daily and walk with Him in the *relationship* made possible by His mercy. Relationship is the context in which we learn to *believe* and *trust* God for the transformation He has promised. In other words, we *enter* God's grace through *faith, trusting* in His ongoing work in our lives (Rom. 5:2).

The question for us to consider is this: Will we embrace the *faith challenge* to enter the grace so needed for a vibrant and fruitful walk with the living God? God invites each of us into this realm of His grace, a realm in which the impossible becomes possible. We come to see that our natural limitations do not prevent us or excuse us from fulfilling God's calling and purposes for our lives. May the Lord open our eyes to *see and believe* that such a life is within our reach, as grace becomes larger in our hearts and more powerful in our lives.

Chapter Two

THE POWER OF GRACE

As we read through the New Covenant Scriptures, we see that the salvation we come into through our faith in Yeshua is one of great victory. One of my favorite verses highlighting this victory takes us back to Romans 5:

> For if by the one man's transgression, death reigned through the one, how much more shall those who receive the overflow of grace and the gift of righteousness reign in life through the One, Messiah Yeshua (Romans 5:17).

This verse serves as a summary statement of verses 15–17, in which Paul contrasts the impact of Adam's sin to the impact of Yeshua's salvation. "One man's transgression" speaks of Adam's sin, resulting in humanity and all creation being infected by death. Because of Adam's sin, death ruled over humanity, and we were powerless to overcome it. The primary result was separation from God and enslavement to sin and death. Every human being is born into this, and nothing we can do in our own power can change our condition. Our own righteous acts, no matter how well intentioned, cannot bring us into the peace with God that every person needs.

Yeshua's victory becomes available to us for overcoming the impact of Adam's sin.

But Paul's point is that Yeshua's salvation changed everything, making it possible for all who would embrace Yeshua as Messiah and Lord to come into a newness of life. Yeshua's victory becomes available to us for overcoming the impact of Adam's sin. Because of Adam's sin, "death reigned" over humanity, but Yeshua's gift of righteousness has an impact that is "much more" than the impact of sin.

WE DO NOT EARN GRACE, WE RECEIVE IT

It can be helpful to consider some key words in this verse. First, Paul refers to *receiving* grace. Those who will *receive* this grace can come into the place of victory he is describing. I think *receiving* is meant here to be a contrast to the idea of *earning* or *deserving* or *striving* for God's blessing. So the idea is that grace is a *gift*, and we can experience it only as we *receive* it, as opposed to deserving it. Thus, all our attempts to *feel worthy* of God's blessing can actually result in our *missing* God's blessing because His blessing is based totally on *His grace*—never on *our worthiness*. Paul wants us to see that *receiving* grace stands in contrast to *feeling* worthy or *achieving* worthiness through our own actions.

Then Paul refers to the *overflow* of this grace. Some translations use the word *abundance*. Numerous Greek lexicons suggest the idea of *super-abundance*. In using this word, Paul is suggesting that there is no shortage of God's grace. His grace is so vast that we cannot come to the end of it. In other words, there is an inexhaustible supply of God's grace for our lives. Its power to change us is "much more" than the power of sin to pull us down, and we must get a revelation of this great truth.

Paul then refers to the *righteousness* imparted to us in salvation. We must see this righteousness, he writes, as a *gift*. This brings us back to the issue of *receiving* rather than *earning* God's grace. Paul highlights this because a gift is not something owed to us. A gift is based totally on the graciousness and generosity of the giver. Thus, a gift is simply to be *received*.

Finally, Paul uses the word *reign*. Recipients of God's gift of righteousness will "reign in life" through Yeshua. Grace brings us into a place of reigning. Clearly, this is to be understood as a victorious position. Reigning can take on many forms, but primarily I think Paul is referring to the issue of sin. Through our connection to Yeshua, instead of sin ruling over us, we are brought into a place of reigning over the sin nature to which we were previously enslaved. Again, it is *grace* that brings us into this place of reigning.

This does not mean we will never sin or fall short. Practically speaking, our place of reigning is something we grow into over the process of a lifetime. The point is that grace makes this victorious process possible. By God's grace, we are no longer enslaved by sin. Adam's "transgression" is no longer the dominant influence on the life of one who has entered this grace through faith.

THE STUMBLING BLOCK OF NATURAL REASONING

Let's consider the process of *receiving* this grace from God. On one hand, the issues I have been highlighting thus far are simple issues, basic to our salvation. Yet we can get tripped up by the very simplicity of it. Honestly, we can stumble over the challenge of simply *receiving* a generous gift we know we do not deserve.

I think the primary hindrance to our *receiving* God's grace is our tendency to focus on ourselves and how *undeserving we are* of God's gift to us. God is so amazingly good and gracious, yet we know we have let Him down far more than we want to think about. Thus, we *do* think about the unworthiness of our own lives. Focusing on how undeserving we are, it becomes *reasonable* to us to consider the idea that "I am just *too* unworthy for God to bless me." When we entertain these thoughts of our unworthiness, what we are actually doing is trying to process God's grace with our *understanding* and our natural *human reasoning*. We *overthink* our unworthiness, and that becomes a stumbling block for simply *receiving* God's grace.

> *We overthink our unworthiness, and that becomes a stumbling block for simply receiving God's grace.*

Now, *are* we undeserving of God's grace? Of course we are! We are not to be in denial about this. The truth is we can never be deserving of this amazing gift of forgiveness and cleansing and the standing of righteousness into which salvation brings us. We can never be deserving of the empowerment provided to us for walking out our calling and destiny. But our undeserving status is the very reason that this is a gift of God's *grace*. Thus, we must look *beyond* what natural reasoning tells us we deserve. That is where grace actually will take us—*beyond* natural reasoning, into a realm to which faith alone can lead us.

Here is the bottom line on this issue: God is *unreasonably* good in how He relates to us. He is unreasonably good in the grace He offers to us, but we often try to process this *un*reasonable goodness with our natural understanding and *reasoning*. Well, how is it even possible for natural reasoning to process what is unreasonable? It is *not* possible. I am reminded of the words of Proverbs 3:5, exhorting us to "trust in Adonai with all your heart, lean not on your own understanding." The Hebrew word here for "trust" is *b'tach*. The idea is to *rely* on or *put our confidence* in the Lord rather than putting confidence in what we can understand. Human understanding or intellect is *incapable* of comprehending God, so we cannot put any confidence in our ability to figure Him out. We are to trust with our *hearts*, which is what *faith* involves. He is far beyond our understanding and far beyond what is reasonable.

So let's come back to the primary stumbling block. As we experience God's goodness and marvel in how gracious He is, we might find ourselves thinking something like this: "I am just trying *understand* how God can be so good to me." Well again, we are trying to *understand* that which is beyond reason. We need to stop trying to understand God's goodness and simply *receive* His blessing as an undeserved gift. The reality is, God is far bigger than what we are capable of understanding. That means we must go *beyond* what we can understand and step into the realm of faith and trust. Only through faith can we enter God's unreasonable goodness and grace. We will never be able to relate to God any other way. We must embrace the call to *trust* God rather than thinking we can somehow figure God out or make sense of His grace.

In Ephesians 1:19, Paul is praying for believers' eyes to be opened for recognizing "what is the immeasurable greatness of (God's) power toward us who believe..." (ESV). In other words, God has released a power in our lives that is beyond our concept of greatness and beyond our ability to measure. Ephesians 3:19 is part of Paul's prayer that believers would come "to know the love of Messiah that surpasses knowledge..." How can we *know* that which is *beyond* knowledge? The

> *Everything about God and His gracious work in our lives is beyond what we are capable of understanding.*

point is, it's not possible for us to really *understand* God's love. The love He has for us is *beyond* what our minds can comprehend. Then in verse 20, he refers to God as doing "far beyond all that we ask or imagine..." God's work in us and through us is *far beyond* anything *we* can even imagine.

In Philippians 4:7, Paul writes of our need to experience the *peace* of God "which surpasses all understanding." In other words, what God makes available to us is a peace that *defies* natural understanding and logic. Similarly, Peter writes of a joy available to us—joy that is "glorious beyond words" (1 Pet. 1:8). The point is, we do not truly have the words to even *describe* this joy God gives us in Yeshua.

Do you see the pattern in these verses? *Everything* about God and His gracious work in our lives is *beyond* what we are capable of understanding. God's work in us goes beyond what makes sense to us.

What, specifically, do we do to try to make grace reasonable? We try to make sense of God's grace by hoping to find something in our lives *deserving* of God's grace. In other words, grace would make sense to us if we could find something in ourselves that makes us worthy. What kinds of things do we look for? Typically, we feel more or less worthy based on how well we are doing in avoiding sin, how often we share our faith with others, and on the quantity and quality of our devotional time with the Lord. The list could go on and on, but His generosity would make sense to our natural thinking if there were something in us that made us feel deserving of His blessing—something in us that God sees and responds to.

But here is the problem: *nothing* in us deserves His generosity, and we *know* this, even though we still try to find something. We want to be able to *feel* worthy so that God's blessing will make sense, but we realize that our own worthiness will always fall short. And so, focusing on ourselves, we end up concluding, based on natural reasoning, that "I'm just too unworthy for God to bless me. It doesn't make sense to me that God would be so good to me. After all that I've done—all the ways I've let God down, all the times I've been self-centered rather than living wholeheartedly for Him. God's goodness to *me* just doesn't make sense." Thinking this way, we lean on our own understanding rather than trusting God for His grace, which is *far bigger* than our understanding.

TOO GOOD TO BE TRUE?

Because we cannot intellectually make sense of grace, we open ourselves up to lies that are rooted in *trying* to make sense of grace. Or we can open ourselves up to lies that try to convince us why grace may be true, but it just doesn't apply to *me* for any number of reasons. These deceptions become believable based on our attempts to make sense of grace, when in fact, it *doesn't* make sense. Grace is far bigger than our minds can ever understand. Grace does not fit into the world of logic and reason.

If we insist on approaching God's grace from the realm of logic and reason, grace will just remain a *concept* to us, an idea that seems too good to be true. Common sense, fueled by the knowledge of our personal shortcomings, convinces us that grace is too good to be true. But if we will go beyond logic and reason and step into the realm of faith, then that which is too good to be true will actually *become* reality for us. Let's be honest about it—grace *really is* too good to be true, yet it *is* true. How can that be possible? It's possible because God's goodness defies logic, reason, and common sense. His grace is far better than the best we can imagine. That is the very reason we must stop trying to make sense of God's grace.

BATTLING THE LIES

There is a daily battle we must face. On one hand, grace is God's *gift* to us. But on the other hand, we actually must *fight* for grace in order to gain access to the blessings of grace. Our fight is against the lies we are tempted to believe when processing grace with our understanding. It's a *fight of faith* that we are involved in. Remember that it is *by faith* that we can *enter into* God's grace, in which we stand (Rom. 5:2). So there are lies rooted in our natural reasoning. We are susceptible to these lies as we attempt to make sense of grace. We must face the task of battling and overcoming those lies daily if we want to enter more *fully into* God's grace.

What are these lies? They can come in many forms, but they typically revolve around thinking our sin is too great for God to forgive. We may think, "I've messed up too many times. I've failed the Lord too many times, and certainly He must be fed up with me. It just makes sense that God has given up on me by now." We may focus on personal feelings of shame or our seeming inability to achieve victory in particular areas of our walk with God. Or we can focus on ways we feel we don't measure up in areas like prayer and fasting. As we focus on transgressions as well as shortcomings, we can conclude that it would be reasonable if God just wrote us off. Again, we are trying to make sense of God's grace. Thinking God's grace must make sense or be reasonable will just lead us to believe the lies.

These are just a few examples, and I could cite many more. Whatever form the lies may take in our lives they leave us feeling disqualified from God's generosity. That is the *reasonable* conclusion we arrive at as we try to make sense of God's grace. But rather than believing the lies, we must battle them, and the most effective weapon we have against these lies is the truth of God's Word and promises. This is part of the process of the renewing of our minds that Paul alludes to in Romans 12:2. The renewing of our minds is a necessary part of the life transformation God is accomplishing in us. Renewing our minds means we learn to *think differently* based on what Yeshua has done for us in salvation. God's Word is what now informs us concerning what is true, even when our experience does not yet match His Word.

Thus, Yeshua's saving work must be our focus when we are otherwise tempted to highlight our own sin or failure. We do not *deny* our shortcomings, but by faith, we see that God's salvation brings a supernatural impartation to us. As we acknowledge our sins and repent, He really does forgive us and cleanse us (more on this in a later chapter). With His Word, we battle the lies daily and are empowered to overcome the downward pull those lies can have on us. Thus, we can enter *by faith* into His grace.

God's grace really does go beyond what *our* minds typically focus on. His love for us defies our logic. Consider the words of Psalm 94:18: "If I say: 'My foot has slipped,' Your mercy, Adonai will hold me up." The Hebrew here for "mercy" is *chesed*, which speaks of God's loving-kindness. In those times when we stumble, God is still holding us up with His love. His love must be our focus in such times. Our stumbling does not override His love, but actually, the reverse is true. His loving-kindness prevails even amid our weakness.

Never forget that Yeshua's righteousness is *much more* powerful to free us than sin's power to hold us down. God gives us grace to bring freedom to our lives. "Those who *receive* abundance of grace…will reign in life through the one, Yeshua the Messiah" (Rom. 5:17). We must remind ourselves daily that God's grace can never be earned or deserved. It can only be received as a gift and entered through faith. Common sense and logic present us with reasons why we would be excluded from God's grace, but we must learn to *receive* from God in spite of the appeals of reason. Remember, grace is unreasonable. It does not make sense.

CHAPTER THREE

GRACE FROM A DIFFERENT PERSPECTIVE

We have been considering the process of receiving God's grace and challenges we face when trying to see God's grace through logic and human reasoning. When we focus on ourselves and the glaring struggles or weaknesses in our lives, we come up with reasons why *we think* God would not want to bless us. Could it be that we are missing something here as we focus on ourselves rather than God? I want to consider an aspect of receiving grace to which we likely need to give more attention.

We usually tend to think about grace from the perspective of *our receiving* what we do not deserve. That is one side of grace, but there is another side. I think we also need to process grace from the perspective of *God giving* what He *loves to give*. So often we unintentionally embrace a "religious" kind of thinking in which we are essentially robbing God of the joy of His Fatherhood. What do I mean by that? Well, think about it. God is the perfect Father, perfect in His generosity and graciousness. He has given a gift to humanity. It is the greatest and most wonderful gift ever given—His Son, Yeshua. In Messiah we are given this amazing access, by faith, into the realm of God's unlimited goodness and generosity. We have access to a grace that is totally beyond what our minds can comprehend. Can we believe that God might actually have *joy* in giving this undeserved gift to man?

JOY IN GIVING

Let's consider an analogy we all can likely relate to. Try to recall a time when you have planned to give a really special gift to someone you love. It may have been as a parent planning a gift for your child, or as a spouse planning a gift for your husband or wife. The principle is the same for anyone who has planned a special gift for a close friend or family member. Try to recall the *joy* of the process. As you were planning the gift, over time, your excitement about *giving* the gift grew. You might have tried to imagine the person's reaction or think about how much the gift will bless the other person. Then the time came when you were finally able to give that person the gift. It made you happy to give that gift to your loved one. So often, the joy of the *giver* is almost greater than the joy of the one *receiving* the gift.

We need to embrace the concept of God enjoying us and having joy in giving us what we don't deserve.

Have you experienced that? We see the joy of someone *receiving* a gift we have planned, and that *gives us* joy. So, what is my point? We need to embrace the concept of *God enjoying* us and having joy in giving us what we don't deserve. Do you *think* of God that way? I truly believe we *should* see God that way. Consider the truth in Scripture that we are created in God's image and likeness. Obviously, God is perfect, and we are quite flawed. Yet the good qualities we may exhibit as people are always a reflection of *perfect* qualities that existed first in God Himself. One of the more positive traits of human nature is the *enjoyment* we have in giving to others. God created us to experience *joy in giving*. Where did that quality come from? It could only have come from God. Man has never done anything good that did not *originate* with God. So, seeing our own tendency to experience joy in giving gives us a glimpse into the heart of God. I believe God receives *joy* in *our receiving* His *gifts* of grace. He has joy in our *enjoyment* of His goodness.

However, "religious" thinking would convince us otherwise. Religious thinking typically sees God from more of a legalistic perspective. Religious thinking usually leads us to a performance orientation in which we hope to be more "acceptable" to God because of our righteous acts. Depending on our personal background, we are all likely influenced to some degree by religious thinking. It can especially affect our concept of what God Himself is like. The religious mindset usually sees God as begrudging in His goodness, but grace truly defies the religious mindset. God Himself does not fit into a religious mode. The prophet Zephaniah tells us something regarding the *heart* of God, even as he was prophesying judgment over Judah: "Adonai your God is in your midst—a mighty Savior! He will delight over you with joy. He will quiet you with His love. He will dance for joy over you with singing" (Zeph. 3:17).

We must guard against religious thinking as it relates to receiving blessings from God. Religious thinking sounds something like this: "Yes, I know God is really good, and I know He loves me, but because *I'm* so *un*worthy, God can't be too happy about blessing me. He can't be too happy about giving the promises of His grace to me freely."

This kind of thinking is a deception. When we believe such lies, we are missing something so important about the very *nature* of God. He has *joy* in *our receiving* His gifts of grace. His joy is in *our receiving* grace, not in our attempts to figure out how we can somehow be *worthy* of it, or our attempts to figure out if we have somehow disqualified ourselves from it.

God has joy as He sees us take hold of that grace that lifts up our lives and takes us beyond our natural limitations. As *we realize* that, yes, grace *really is working* in us, I believe that gives

God great pleasure. God gives us grace for a simple reason: He *loves to be gracious!* He loves to show generosity to us. In the writings of the Hebrew prophet Micah, we read, "He will not retain His anger forever, because He delights in mercy" (Micah 7:18).

Do you see this? According to this verse, God actually *has pleasure* in showing mercy to undeserving people. That's His nature. So, if it's His nature, He must experience a *joy* in defying logic and giving us what we don't deserve. When we overthink our unworthiness, I believe we rob God of that joy. But recognizing God's desire to *be* gracious can help us *overcome* the doubts and questions we struggle with regarding our own worthiness.

RECEIVING LIKE A CHILD

Coming back to the analogy of giving and receiving a gift, I would like to consider another side to the analogy. I think we can see a characteristic in children that gives us insight into the nature of receiving. If you are a parent and/or a grandparent, let me ask you a question. In giving gifts to your younger children or grandchildren, when was the last time they responded by telling you they were unworthy? "Oh no, I couldn't receive this gift. I really don't deserve it." Have you ever experienced this? I didn't think so. Neither have I. In fact, even with adults, *we* might respond to someone giving us a gift, saying something like, "Oh, you shouldn't have," or "Oh, you didn't have to do that." But more often than not we will still gladly accept the gift. Usually, if we *do* offer a brief protest, it's just a religious mindset that makes us struggle with *simply receiving.* But again, we will still likely accept the gift.

A big difference between children and adults in this area is that children do not offer *any* "religious" pretense of being undeserving. Young children just do not think that way. They do not protest that the gift is unnecessary. Of course it's unnecessary! It's a *gift*, not a payment! Children do not make any attempt to bring *logic* or *worthiness* into the picture. They don't make any attempt to *justify* receiving the gift they've just been given. This is just how children are made up, and really, it's part of how *we* are made up as children of God. But too often we as adults process *God's* gifts and blessings with logic and reason rooted in religious thinking. There is certainly a place for logic and reason in our walk with God, but in this area of receiving His undeserved grace we must get out from the realm of logic and reason and step into the realm of faith, trust, and gratitude.

We need to become childlike in embracing God's gifts.

We need to become childlike in embracing God's gifts. We need to nurture this child-likeness because it does not come naturally to us as we "grow" out of our childhood years. Perhaps the best way we can nurture this childlike faith is to make a point of spending time every day simply thanking God for a goodness that we don't deserve. Daily, we can *praise Him, remind ourselves* that His grace is neither logical nor reasonable, and give Him thanks for that.

Grace is not just about *me* and *my need.* That might sound strange, but I do believe it's a true statement. Grace is also about God having opportunity to *express* His nature and His generosity. And yes, He has joy in our receiving His generosity.

THE TESTIMONY OF GRACE

There is yet another side to consider in receiving grace from God. We can gain insight from Paul's first letter to his disciple, Timothy:

> Trustworthy is the saying and deserving of complete acceptance: 'Messiah Yeshua came into the world to save sinners'—of whom I am foremost. Yet for this reason I was shown mercy—so that in me as the foremost, Messiah Yeshua might demonstrate His complete patience, as an example for those about to put their trust in Him for eternal life (1 Timothy 1:15–16).

Think about what Paul is saying here. He refers to himself as "foremost" among sinners. In today's vocabulary, we might say he was in *first place* among those deserving God's displeasure and judgment. But he understood something about a particular aspect of God showing mercy. Paul saw that *he* received mercy as an *example* for *others* to be able to *see* how gracious God is on behalf of people who are undeserving.

Before he had his encounter with Yeshua, Paul was violent in his rage and opposition against believers. Perhaps this is why he saw himself as "foremost" among sinners, but if God could have mercy on *him*, He could have mercy on anyone. Paul realized that his own life was meant to be a *testimony* of the grace of God. His life was to be a testimony in which *others* would be able to see how good and generous God is.

Grace received becomes a powerful testimony, as God displays His amazing goodness in the lives of undeserving people.

I suspect that *seeing* this principle was key to Paul not getting tripped up by the evils of his past. I imagine he had to work through feelings of guilt and condemnation after he had come to faith in Yeshua. I don't say that with certainty because Paul did not write about those particular struggles, but I suspect he did have to work through such issues. Yet the consistent testimony we see throughout his writings is that Paul fully embraced forgiveness and cleansing from the Lord. He *knew* he was forgiven. He *knew* the truth and power of God's grace in his life.

Dear friend, grace *received* becomes a powerful testimony, as God *displays* His amazing goodness in the lives of undeserving people. The issue should never be, "How can I be worthy of it?" Rather, it's all about the simple question of, "Will I *receive* it as a gift and then *enjoy and appreciate* it as a gift? Will I allow my life, as I *receive* this gift, to be a testimony to others of the generosity, goodness, and power of God to transform needy lives?"

Thus, we see three basic perspectives for receiving God's grace:

1. **We *desperately need* His grace.** There is no other way for us grow in our walk with God. There is no other way for us to fulfill our calling and destiny in God. There is no other way for us to live beyond our human limitations, and that is what we are called to do. *We need* God's grace.

2. ***God's nature* is to be gracious and generous.** He experiences joy in giving us a gift we do not deserve.

3. **A life impacted by grace becomes a glorious *testimony* of the goodness of God.** His mercy is on display through the lives of undeserving believers.

Grace is about *us* and *our need*. Grace is about *God* and *His joy* in being gracious. And grace is about *others seeing* God's goodness through the testimony of our lives.

THE IMPACT OF GRACE

While there are *many* ways God impacts our lives with His grace, I think we could say that there is a *foundational* work of His grace summed up in Romans 14:17. There, we read that "the kingdom of God is…*righteousness* and *peace* and *joy* in the Holy Spirit" (NKJV, italics added). A grace-filled work of the Spirit of God produces in us a righteousness we do not deserve, peace beyond comprehension, and joy beyond description. Again, these are not the only expressions of grace in our lives, but they represent a foundational work of grace, building blocks for moving forward and growing in our walk with the Lord.

When we speak of this Kingdom inheritance of righteousness, peace, and joy in the Holy Spirit, it can almost sound like a self-serving "feel-good" emphasis. But actually, the opposite is true. These qualities are all about us being *free and empowered* to represent Yeshua and His Kingdom to the world around us.

Consider some of the mindsets and tendencies that stand in opposition to these qualities of righteousness, peace, and joy. Some that come to mind are condemnation, shame, anxiety, fear, worry, discouragement, and hopelessness. The enemy of our souls intends these negative mindsets, and many more like them, to leave us self-absorbed in our failures, our fears, and our trials. If we are focused largely on ourselves, we will feel like we have little to give to a needy world. However, God intends for righteousness, peace, and joy in the Spirit to lift us *out* of our self-focus. He wants to propel us into a life of spiritual growth and fruitfulness as we live to bless others and to represent the Lord to a world in desperate need.

Righteousness enables us to have an intimate *relationship* with the Lord. It's only through relationship with God that we can fully discover our destiny and the reason we are alive. As those made righteous, we also can experience the indwelling presence of the Holy Spirit, empowering us for a fruitful life. *Peace* is a supernatural work of the Spirit that *steadies* us amid the storms of life that can leave us feeling anxious or fearful. We can know peace, even as the world around us experiences shaking. And *joy* brings an *energizing* to our hearts, as we experience the many challenges of living for God's Kingdom purposes.

In the chapters that follow, we will explore each of these supernatural Kingdom qualities and consider the role of grace in experiencing them.

CHAPTER FOUR

THE GIFT OF RIGHTEOUSNESS

A s we considered in chapter 2, Paul identifies God's "gift of righteousness" as a foundational blessing of His grace (Rom. 5:17). What does it mean when the Bible says we have been given this gift of righteousness? It points to the fact that, as we receive Yeshua and repent of our sins, we are fully *forgiven* as well as inwardly *cleansed* of unrighteousness. By God's grace, Yeshua's own righteousness is imparted to us.

Many refer to this as *positional* righteousness, meaning that, because our lives are by faith "positioned" in Yeshua, *His* perfect righteousness is accounted to us, even though we still fall short. While this is true, I believe the gift of righteousness goes even further. Our *position* of righteousness in connection with Yeshua allows us to receive the Spirit of God in our own lives, thus *empowering* us for a walk that expresses God's righteous ways. We do not live this out perfectly. Yeshua was the only man who could do that. However, we do experience the empowerment of the Spirit. As we live in deepening relationship and walk in a growing dependence on God, our lives *reflect* the beauty of His holiness more fully.

When we do stumble or fall short our fellowship with God is hindered. By God's grace we can confess our sin, turn from it (repent), and immediately return to fellowship with Him. From the place of fellowship with God, we are empowered for righteous living. I like to think of this righteousness imparted to us as a *dynamic* righteousness, not simply positional. It is dynamic in the sense that righteousness is actively *working* in us by God's Spirit, empowering us for the life of obedience and holiness.

> *Righteousness is actively working in us by God's Spirit, empowering us for the life of obedience and holiness.*

THE PROBLEM WITH SIN

Again, it is *sin* that interferes with the work of righteousness in us. As believers, we have placed our trust in the death and resurrection of Yeshua. Thus, we have access to God's forgiveness, as well as freedom from sin's power to rule us. Although we, in Yeshua, are free from sin's *authority*, we are not yet free from sin's *influence*. Living in mortal bodies and a fallen world, we find that we can still be drawn by sin's allurement. Of course, when Yeshua returns, we will receive glorious, new, resurrected bodies. Until that time, we are still attracted in various ways to attitudes and actions that lead us to go our own way rather than God's. That is at the heart of what sin is—choosing our own way and rejecting God's ways.

Our strength in battling temptation lies in the power of our ongoing *relationship* with God as we look to Him for the grace and power to resist temptation. Remember, God is at work in our lives, by His Spirit, to bring forth in us a likeness to Yeshua. This is what we were made for, but sin interferes with this dynamic work of the Spirit. Sin prevents us from coming into the very purpose for which we are created: to know God, to love Him, and to represent who God is to a lost and needy world.

THE DOORWAY

As sin interferes with our ongoing relationship with the Lord, it is essential that we learn to receive and walk in the fullness of *forgiveness* that God makes available to us in Yeshua. This is a major issue for us because receiving forgiveness is actually the doorway into everything God wants to do in our lives. Everything in our walk with the Lord begins with forgiveness. We must embrace the reality and power of forgiveness so that it is much more than just an idea or doctrine. God's forgiveness is what I would call the *overlooked miracle* in the life of every believer. As you read further, it will become clearer what I mean by that.

As essential as forgiveness is for a fruitful and growing walk with God, the truth is, we as believers can often find ourselves struggling to *receive* this work of God's grace. Remember, we struggle with receiving grace as we try to *process* grace with our natural thinking. But as we have considered, God's grace is unreasonable, so our minds challenge the grace of God in many ways. That is why grace must become *revelation* to us, so we will not be slaves to the struggle of our minds to *receive* grace.

The struggle goes something like this—as we mentally process God's promises in our lives we can find our minds or natural reasoning presenting an inward "argument" *against* faith and trusting. Natural reasoning, of course, is informed by facts, feelings, and circumstances. Faith is informed by God's Word and promises, in spite of circumstances often contradicting the promise. *Faith* is what embraces and receives God's grace, looking beyond the fact that grace does not make sense. As our minds struggle with receiving grace, an inward argument develops between faith and natural thinking. Or we could say, the argument is between receiving grace from God rather than feeling guilt and condemnation for our sins and shortcomings. We receive grace by faith, while guilt and condemnation flow out of natural reasoning and emotion.

Grace must "win the argument" over our mind and emotions if we want to walk in our destiny in God. We must learn to fully receive God's grace, and that begins with *fully* receiving God's *forgiveness*.

FAITHFUL AND JUST

Let's consider a key verse that many learn as new believers. 1 John 1:9 instructs us as follows: "If we confess our sins, He is faithful and just to forgive us our sins and to cleanse us from all unrighteousness" (NKJV). This verse is meant to give us confidence that we really are forgiven when we acknowledge our sins to God. Let's unpack the verse a bit because the full picture of what John is telling us here is quite powerful.

The verse emphasizes two key points about our walk with God and the power of His salvation in our lives. First, when we sin, we are to *confess* it, which simply means that we state to God our *agreement* with Him that we have done something wrong and desire His forgiveness. John's point is that when we confess our sin, we are fully *forgiven*. Second, he writes that we are *cleansed* of all unrighteousness. We must understand something important here. Our experience of forgiveness and cleansing is based on *who God* is. In other words, when we confess our sins, the reason we can be fully confident in *being* forgiven and cleansed is because *God* is faithful, and *God* is just. He is *faithful* to show us mercy, and He is *just* in bringing cleansing to our lives. It is not an issue of *my worthiness* but *His faithfulness*.

FORGIVENESS IS DIFFERENT FROM CLEANSING

So God *forgives* and God *cleanses*. Are these just two different words used to say the same thing? No, they are different, and both forgiveness *and* cleansing are needed in our lives. Here is the reason why. When you confess your sin, if you understand that God *forgives* you, but you figure that God still sees you as a misfit because you keep falling short, there is a problem. You may think, "Yes, I know I'm forgiven, but I figure God *must* be pretty frustrated or upset with me because I seem to keep blowing it in my walk with Him." If you process things that way, then you are not understanding the power of forgiveness and cleansing. Let's consider this.

Based on 1 John 1:9, the moment we confess our sin and ask God to forgive us, He forgives us. There is no sense from the verse that there must be a certain amount of *time* that passes before we can *feel* forgiven. We do not have to put ourselves on "spiritual probation" until we feel more welcomed by God. There is no sense here or anywhere else in the Bible that we must do anything more than *confess* our sin. Yes, we need to be sincere, truly sorry for what we have done.

We need to hate our sin (not our*selves*, but the sin), and our intent should always be to turn from that sin (repentance) and by God's grace not go back to it. Specific heart attitudes must go along with our confession or else the confession will be empty. The moment we sincerely confess our sin and ask forgiveness, God does

> *We do not have to put ourselves on "spiritual probation" until we feel more welcomed by God.*

it. He forgives us. There is no "waiting period" we must go through before we can "feel" forgiven.

However, we can sometimes *struggle* with feeling forgiven, even when we have confessed our sin. After confessing, we can find ourselves thinking something like, "What can I say or do so that God will know I really mean it?" We might not actually verbalize that question, yet we can have the tendency to want to "add" something to feel like our confession will be more meaningful. We struggle to *simply receive* the forgiveness and cleansing that God promises. We struggle because we lose sight of the fact that God is faithful and just.

In this process the enemy tries to convince us of two key lies, both related to God's *faithfulness* to forgive and God's *justness* in cleansing us. How does he get us to believe the lies? By drawing our focus more to ourselves and our shortcomings rather than to God and His grace. Let's consider the forgiveness issue first.

DON'T BELIEVE THE LIES

The lies we are tempted with can take on many forms. The basic idea is, "I've sinned too many times" or "I just can't seem to get it right, since I keep stumbling over and over in the same area." Another lie is, "My sin is too terrible—too unclean—and I feel so embarrassed and ashamed; I *can't see* how God could just forgive me." These are just a few examples. There are many variations on these kinds of thoughts, but they take us to the "logical" conclusion that, "What *I am* or what *I've done* goes beyond what is reasonable for God to forgive. How can I really believe that God forgives me?" Well, what John is pointing to is the fact that we can believe God's forgiveness for the simple reason that *God is faithful*. He is *faithful* to forgive us. He is *faithful* to offer us a mercy we don't deserve.

If we focus primarily on how bad our sin is, or how often we have stumbled, or how bad we feel about ourselves, we will never be able to believe we are forgiven. John's point is that it's *not about* you and me and how deserving we are—it's all about *God's faithfulness* to be merciful, and that changes everything. If we think, "I just don't see how God could possibly forgive me," then we are not grasping how *faithful* God is to show mercy.

Paul tells us in Romans 3:3 that God's faithfulness can never be outdone by man's *un*faithfulness. This tells us that no matter how bad we are (or *think* we are), God's faithfulness will be greater than our *un*faithfulness. The book of Lamentations gives us tremendous encouragement in this regard:

> But this I call to mind, and therefore I have hope: The steadfast love of the Lord never ceases; his mercies never come to an end; they are new every morning; great is your faithfulness (Lamentations 3:21–23, ESV).

Consider the writer's description here. First, he cites the steadfast *love* of God. He says that we can never reach the end of it. His love never runs dry. So even when we sin and fall short, God never stops loving us. The next statement takes things further. His *mercies*, as well, never come to an end. His merciful disposition to *forgive* can never come to an end. You and I *cannot sin enough* to reach the end of God's mercy. Of course, that does not give us license to just go ahead and sin. Paul addresses that heresy in Romans 6. However, we can never reach the point where God would say, "That's it! I have no more mercy left for you."

Why? It's because of who God is—"great is *Your* faithfulness." God's *faithfulness* is related here to His *mercy*, and that is the basis for *knowing* we are forgiven. It's not because *we deserve* mercy. It's because *God is faithful* to *be* merciful. The writer says, "This I call to mind..." What is it *you* are calling to mind when you have fallen short? Is it your unworthiness? Or is it God's faithfulness? Calling to mind our shortcomings will just lead to discouragement, but calling to mind God's faithfulness will strengthen our faith to *believe* His unreasonable mercy.

> *You and I cannot sin enough to reach the end of God's mercy.*

God is *faithful* to forgive us. We can *count* on Him to show mercy and forgive, regardless of how *badly* we have messed up, or how *many times* we have stumbled. Not only that, but His mercies are *new every morning*. It's God's mercy that greets us as we awaken to every new day. His mercies just keep coming back, day after day. You cannot shake it, and you cannot outrun it. His mercy is what greets us every morning, so we might as well just believe it and embrace it. I encourage you to get in the habit of thanking God every day, knowing that He has *new* mercies for you for each day.

I appreciate the ESV translation of Isaiah 30:18: "Therefore the Lord waits to be gracious to you, and therefore he exalts himself to show mercy to you." Think about that. The greatness of God's character is actually magnified as He *shows us mercy*. Hopefully, seeing His mercy from that perspective can help us realize that it is a *righteous* thing for us to *trust* God's forgiveness because it *honors God* when we receive His mercy. We can fully trust in God's forgiveness, not because we have *loved Him* perfectly, but because *He loves us* perfectly, and His mercy is rooted in His compassion and His steadfast love that never comes to an end.

Now, there is a second lie related to 1 John 1:9. John writes that God is *just* in bringing cleansing to our lives once we have confessed our sin. This is something we can struggle with because, if God *cleanses* us that means He actually removes from us all traces of sin and uncleanness. We are tempted to think that, after having just sinned, "How can I be clean by simply confessing and repenting?" The answer is because it's a *supernatural* process we are part of in our relationship with the Lord. It's a *supernatural* work God does in us through the power of salvation, and His cleansing, as well, is a supernatural work.

Paul uses different wording to make the same point in Romans 3:26, where he writes that God is "just and the justifier…" of those who put their trust in Yeshua's righteousness. In other words, God is *just* in *justifying* you and me. *Justify* simply means to declare us righteous and clean in His sight. God is *just* in declaring us righteous. It's not a violation of His righteous justice to make us clean. And so, no matter how unclean we may *feel* when we have sinned, if we will confess our sin from a sincere heart, He really does *remove* the uncleanness from our lives. We can struggle to believe this because it just seems *too easy*, but that is a wrong way to see things.

In no way is forgiveness too easy. For Yeshua to die on the cross was not easy. But He paid a great price so that we would be able to *trust* in His forgiveness and cleansing.

THE RAMIFICATIONS OF OUR CLEANSING

This is the truth that is so difficult for us to believe: in Yeshua, we are now clean in God's eyes and *He sees* no unrighteousness in us. That does not mean we don't still sin. It means God *sees* us as being cleansed through Yeshua when we *confess* our sin. We can think, "Well, maybe God does forgive me, but I'm sure He must be keeping track of all the ways I've fallen short." Such thinking makes sense to us, but it contradicts God's Word.

Psalm 130:3–4 should encourage us: "If You, Adonai, kept a record of iniquities—my Lord, who could stand? For with You there is forgiveness, so You may be revered." We read in 2 Corinthians 5:19 that God is *not counting* our sins against us. He is not keeping a record of our failures. If I am *forgiven* but not *cleansed*, then my sin remains. Yet God's Word is clear that there is *no record* of our sin, so the only way that is possible is if we are cleansed as well as forgiven.

Another thought we can be tempted with is, "Yes, God forgives me, but He still must see me as a messed-up failure." This, too, is a lie from the enemy. If we believe God sees us as failures and misfits then we cannot help but wonder if, at some point, God will just give up on us. The truth of our redemption in Yeshua goes far beyond what makes sense to us. In Yeshua, God removes from our lives all that is deserving of judgment. He does not just overlook it. He *removes* it. Honestly, there is no way our natural minds can make sense of this, and that is why we must see it by faith.

Let me use a little different wording to bring out another side of this issue. When we consider our attitudes or actions and how we have fallen short of God's righteousness, our inward sense of justice leaves us unsettled by the *simplicity* of this process of receiving forgiveness. We struggle to be *at peace* with the idea of being totally forgiven and cleansed, just by confessing our sin. We should remind ourselves of the words of Isaiah 53, the clearest description in the Hebrew Scriptures of the saving work of Messiah. In verse 5, we read, "But He was wounded for our transgressions, He was bruised for our iniquities; the chastisement for our peace was upon Him, and by His stripes we are healed" (NKJV).

Note the wording here. The chastisement, or punishment, *for our peace* was upon Him (Yeshua). So, upon Yeshua was the punishment intended to bring *peace* to you and me. Well, when we sin and are truly sorry, we feel like we should be punished. But *Yeshua* took our punishment upon Himself, and God intended for that to bring *us* into a place of *peace*. We don't have to have *any doubt* about our forgiveness. We can be totally at peace with God Himself, and with the *concept* that God forgives us and makes us clean and righteous. Regardless of what logic and reason tell us, we don't have to doubt our forgiveness or be unsettled about it.

So here is a question each of us must answer: "Am I *at peace* with being forgiven, as Isaiah 53 suggests I should be?" We can *be* at peace only as we accept forgiveness as a gift and not try to feel deserving of it.

UNFORGIVABLE?

One summer back in the 1980s, our congregation, Beth Messiah Congregation, had a weeklong outreach campaign. During that week, teams went into the streets, subway stops, and parks throughout the Washington, DC area. We engaged in many quality conversations with probably thousands of people.

I can remember clearly that so many folks we spoke with felt they could not receive salvation. It was not because they didn't believe in Jesus or didn't want to have a relationship with God. But they were convinced that their own sins and the unworthiness of their lives was too great for God to forgive them. A common response was, "After all I've done? I just can't see how God could forgive me." How tragic it is that the devil has successfully convinced so many people that their sin is greater than God's mercy. This is a demonic lie that has afflicted believers and unbelievers alike.

I love what is written in Psalm 103, where David writes, "Bless Adonai, O my soul, and forget not all His benefits: He forgives all your iniquity..." (v. 2–3). The Hebrew word translated as *iniquity* is *ah-von*, which speaks of more than just weakness or stumbling—it speaks of wickedness. And yes, God forgives it all.

I think we need to remind ourselves regularly of the *supernatural nature* of the forgiveness and cleansing we have received. Romans 4:5 says that He is the God who "justifies the ungodly..." God makes the *ungodly* righteous, yet He Himself is holy and just. How do we understand this? It's a supernatural work that does not make sense to our natural minds. We must see forgiveness and cleansing as a *supernatural* work rather than a *logical* work, or else we won't be able to fully *receive* forgiveness and be at *peace* with the idea of *being* forgiven. We will struggle to receive it because it's not logical or reasonable to our natural thinking. By faith we can receive forgiveness as a supernatural miracle of God's grace.

For the ungodly to be made righteous—for you and me to be forgiven and cleansed—is as much a miracle as healing the sick and raising the dead. It's not as spectacular, but it's just as great a miracle. How else could an *ungodly* person be *made righteous?* We must *see* forgiveness as a *supernatural* transaction that has nothing to do with what we reasonably deserve. *Faith* is the only way we can receive it, and that frees us from having to somehow *make sense* of forgiveness.

God is *faithful* in forgiving us, and He is *just* in cleansing us. We can *count* on being forgiven because God is *faithful*, and He never runs out of mercy. And then, we can be *confident* in our cleansing, in spite of how we may *feel* about ourselves, because God is *just* in cleansing us and removing our guilt. That means God Himself sees us as righteous and clean. Thus, He has no intention of giving up on us at times when we stumble. He cleanses us and makes us righteous because He is bringing us into a destiny, and He does not intend to give up on us.

> *The idea that God must be unjust or irresponsible to see you and me as righteous and clean is a lie from the enemy.*

The idea that God must be unjust or irresponsible to see you and me as righteous and clean is a lie from the enemy. It is meant to take away our confidence that God sees us as clean, even in our times of struggling. God's Word says He is *just* in declaring us holy and without blame, and *we* must be *seeing ourselves* in the same way. Seeing this truth is really the only way we can have hope for our future and destiny in God. If God merely *overlooks* our sin, but then leaves us still guilty and unclean, we are left with no hope. Why? Because it's our *cleansing* that enables us to see that we are free to move forward into our calling and destiny, without being weighed down and held back by our sins and failures.

In those times when you have blown it, and you are struggling to get out of feeling like a failure—struggling to believe His forgiveness, struggling to trust that your life really is on a path of righteousness—remind yourself that God is *faithful* to forgive you, and He is *just* in cleansing you and calling you righteous.

EXAMPLES TO FOLLOW

One of the great heroes of the Bible is King David. David was a very flawed individual. We know of his love for God and the great victories he won, but we also know of his sins, including adultery and murder. Yet, consider his words from Psalm 18:

> He (Adonai) brought me out to a wide-open place. He rescued me since He delighted in me. Adonai rewarded me for my righteousness. For the cleanness of my hands He repaid me. For I kept the ways of Adonai, and did not turn wickedly from my God (Psalm 18:20–22).

After some of the terrible things David had done, how could he think that God saw him as righteous? The answer is simple: David understood the miracle of forgiveness and cleansing. He understood the miracle of God's grace. In reading some of his writings, we might be tempted to wonder if he lived in denial, but that is not the case. Although David had major moral failures in his life, he was a man who embraced the walk of repentance. As we look at David's life and read his writing, it appears that once David confessed his sin, he never rehearsed it again.

Similarly, we might consider Saul of Tarsus, or the apostle Paul. He had sinned greatly against the Lord and against the early believers in Judea. Yet he wrote in 1 Corinthians 4:4, "For

I know of nothing against myself…" He fully received forgiveness and grace to the point that nothing of his past held him back or weighed him down. I suspect that in his early years as a believer, he probably had to work through much guilt. Even in his later years, I would imagine he felt sadness for the things he did. But Paul did not let his past sins weigh him down. Why? Because he knew the God who delights in being merciful.

Neither David nor Paul lived in denial. Rather, they had a *revelation* of the miracle of God's forgiveness and cleansing. That revelation was so powerful in their lives that it truly did wipe away the guilt and the consciousness of the terrible sins of their past. We must have a revelation of God's forgiveness *and* cleansing. Otherwise the enemy's lies concerning the hopelessness of our lives become reasonable and believable to us.

RELEASED *FROM* AND RELEASED *INTO*

Let me share one last thought on forgiveness and cleansing. Forgiveness releases us *from* something, while cleansing releases us *into* something.

As God forgives us we are released *from* the guilt and punishment our sins deserve. God lifts *from* us the burden of condemnation that keeps us trapped in a hopelessness that leaves us unable to believe God would want to have relationship with us or use us for His glory.

I believe we could say that cleansing, on the other hand, releases us *into* something. It releases us *into* God's ongoing work to cause our lives to be conformed to Yeshua's likeness. Cleansing releases us *into* a walk of increasing holiness and *into* greater measures of our calling and destiny. God's cleansing is what positions us to experience that work of God to do in us what is beyond anything we can ask or think.

Psalm 149:4 says, "For the Lord takes pleasure in His people; He will beautify the humble with salvation" (NKJV). God's cleansing in our lives is part of His work of "beautifying" us. We should remind ourselves daily that God is at work in us to make us beautiful, by the power of His salvation. He inwardly beautifies us so we will shine as lights in a world needing His love and mercy. He beautifies us as He takes away our sin and our shame. He also "takes pleasure" in us, even as we are still in the *process* of becoming like Yeshua.

Psalm 34:5 says, "Those who look to him (the Lord) are radiant, and their faces shall never be ashamed" (ESV). Focusing on ourselves, we cannot help but end up feeling guilty and ashamed. By focusing on Him and the undeserved mercy and grace He gives us, we become radiant. That is the impact of this grace that so defies our logic and understanding.

CHAPTER FIVE

THE CONDEMNATION COUNTERFEIT

As we discussed in chapter 4, God's gift of righteousness is the beginning point of His work of grace in our lives. As we *receive* His forgiveness and cleansing that becomes a foundation for God to continue to work in our lives in different ways in which we need His grace. Forgiveness becomes the doorway for God to use us and bring us into our calling and destiny. It is also the doorway into the walk of holiness to which we aspire. For this reason, I believe much of the *devil's* focus in our life is aimed at drawing us into unbelief regarding our forgiveness. If we do not believe we are forgiven we will not move forward in our believing life. The main tool the devil uses to keep us from embracing God's forgiveness is *condemnation*. I would define *condemnation* as a nagging sense of guilt and uncleanness, leaving us feeling that God must be displeased with us, even though we have confessed our sin with a sincere heart.

CONDEMNATION DISTANCES US FROM GOD

Condemnation will typically lead us to keep ourselves "at a distance" from God, rather than *pursuing* Him in relationship. There certainly are other reasons we stay distant from the Lord, especially at times when we are not willing to repent of sinful actions. But our focus here is on times when we *do* repent, yet we distance ourselves from Him.

Why do we do this? Because condemnation leaves us feeling unwelcome in His presence. We distance ourselves from God because we believe the lie that He wants nothing to do with us. Yet, it's only *in His presence* that we can be *empowered* for the obedience we know we have fallen short of. We cannot possibly grow in godliness if we live our lives apart from His presence. Thus, we put ourselves in a no-win situation when we distance ourselves from Him. Condemnation is one of the great enemies of the work of God's grace in our lives. It has the effect of essentially nullifying God's work of grace in us.

Condemnation blinds us to the grace of God.

With condemnation there is a highlighting of God's displeasure as being greater than His mercy. Sadly, we are all susceptible to this as believers, regardless of how long we have been walking with the Lord. We will be especially susceptible to condemnation as we live with hearts and minds that want to *pursue* a deep relationship with Him. When we live with that desire for deep and growing relationship with the Lord we rightly set a high standard for our lives, based on the purity, holiness, and fruitfulness we desire. Thus, we can actually become *more susceptible* to condemnation because we can clearly see how we fall short of the standards we set. The more we yearn in our hearts to *be like* Yeshua and to live a life that honors Him, the more clearly we will see the ways we fall short. As we set a standard that is high, it can be easy to find ourselves not measuring up. Not measuring up *can* lead us down a path where we end up feeling condemned and like we are letting God down.

Condemnation can certainly be related to blatant sin, but it can also be related to simply falling short of healthy *expectations* we have set for our walk with God. We may set goals for our prayer life or for fasting or other areas of spiritual disciplines, but then we get down on ourselves as we see ways we have *not met* those goals.

For example, we might set a goal to pray for an hour a day, but then we can regularly find ourselves distracted after five minutes and we give up. Being disappointed with ourselves, we then open ourselves to the lie that *God* is disappointed with us as well. Ultimately, condemnation *blinds* us to the grace of God. It is contrary to everything God wants to do in our lives.

NO CONDEMNATION?

Paul makes some powerful definitive statements related to condemnation in Romans 8:

> Therefore, there is now *no condemnation* for those who are in Messiah Yeshua. For the law of the Spirit of life in Messiah Yeshua has set you free from the law of sin and death (Romans 8:1-2, italics added).

> What then shall we say in view of these things? If God is for us, who can be against us? He who did not spare His own Son but gave Him up for us all, how shall He not also with Him freely give us all things? *Who shall bring a charge* against God's elect? It is God who justifies. *Who is the one who condemns?* It is Messiah, who died, and moreover was raised, and is now at the right hand of God and who also intercedes for us (Romans 8:31–34, italics added).

As I read these passages I am struck by the fact that Paul *begins and ends* Romans 8 with strong statements on the reality of *freedom* from condemnation for those who are "in Messiah." Later, I explain *why* I think he did that because I think it is significant. But let's consider what Paul tells us in verse 1. Notice it does not say there that God does not condemn us.

What it actually says is that there *is no* condemnation for those in Messiah, suggesting that condemnation itself is a deception for anyone whose life is in Messiah. That does not mean we never sin or fall short. It means that, by faith, we recognize that God Himself *sees* us as those whose lives are now *connected* to Yeshua and His perfect righteousness.

His righteousness becomes *our* righteousness. So when we *do* fall short in some way and the Holy Spirit convicts us, as we *respond* to that conviction with sincere confession and repentance, in *God's* eyes, our guilt is taken away. That means, in *our* eyes, condemnation is to be removed. There *is no* condemnation for those who are in Messiah Yeshua.

At the end of the chapter, Paul strengthens his point about freedom from condemnation by asking and answering two questions: "Who shall bring a charge against (us)?" and then, "Who is the one who condemns (us)?" The answers he gives are meant to settle the issue. If God, the holy and righteous Creator, has declared us to be righteous, *no one* can bring any charge against us that has merit. If Yeshua, the sinless Messiah and Son of God, gave His life for us and now intercedes on our behalf at the Father's right hand, *no one* can condemn us. Only a righteous one has authority to condemn someone else before God.

Consider Yeshua's words in John 8, as He encountered a group of religious leaders preparing to stone a woman caught in adultery. He said to them, "The sinless one among you, let him be the first to throw a stone at her" (John 8:7). Again, the principle is clear—only one who is righteous has authority to condemn another before God. Yeshua, the only perfectly righteous man who ever lived, has chosen not to condemn us as we deserve, but to *intercede* on our behalf. Paul's point in Romans 8 is that condemnation has no place in the life of a repentant believer. When we do give place to condemnation, we are essentially passing judgment on ourselves. But God Himself is the *only* righteous judge, and He has declared us *not guilty* in Messiah. In His mercy, in response to our faith in Yeshua, He overrides the judgment we know we deserve.

Why, then, do we still find ourselves *feeling* condemnation? There are many reasons, but I believe it is often rooted in our personal sense of justice. We sin or fall short in some way, and our basic sense of justice tells us that we *should* be punished. It's really too good to be true to think that the punishment *we deserve* has been totally taken by Yeshua. We end up *taking on* the punishment we feel we deserve, as we get down on ourselves.

> *Condemnation is a counterfeit influence—a false guide—that keeps us from fully seeing the power of the cross.*

Condemnation becomes our way of self-punishment for how we are disappointed in ourselves and how we believe we have disappointed God. Condemnation seeks to convince us that there is no calling for us, and that God could never use us for His glory. Why? Because we let God down and failed Him too many times. If we buy into this kind of thinking, we are basically concluding that *sin* has a more powerful impact on our lives than *grace*.

CONDEMNATION IS A FALSE GUIDE

Ultimately, condemnation is what I call a *counterfeit influence*—a false guide—that keeps us from fully seeing the power of the cross, where Yeshua laid down His life for us. It's not that condemnation is based on inaccuracies because we really *have* fallen short of God's righteous ways. That's why condemnation is believable to us. Of course, the deception of condemnation is that our *sin* becomes the final word in *defining* our lives. It ignores the redemptive and restorative power of the cross, and *God* intends for *His redemption* to be the final word in defining us.

When we walk in condemnation, we ultimately strip the cross of its *power to save*, and we end up reducing our salvation to a theory—an idea that lacks real power. We would never *say* that because we do affirm the *idea* of the power of salvation, but we can deny its power *in us* through what we ultimately choose to believe. If I stand guilty, in spite of my trusting in Yeshua for my salvation, then essentially, *I am* stripping the cross of its power to *change me*. Remember, the cross of Yeshua does not simply picture a noble act that *inspires* us to righteous living. The cross is the power of God *unto* salvation (Rom. 1:17). It *empowers* us for a victorious life, but condemnation deceives us and robs us of salvation's victory.

Yeshua gave His life on the cross, providing a *new starting point* for us. Obviously, we *were* guilty, but when we put our trust in the shed blood of our sinless Messiah, our guilt was taken away. Yeshua has freed us by giving His life for us, a huge price that was paid on our behalf. But it's a huge price with huge *results* because as we submit our lives to the Lord and receive His life in return, our guilt is taken away. There *is* no condemnation. Thus, condemnation becomes a false guide, steering us away from the Lord Himself.

THE LORD IS OUR TRUE GUIDE

If condemnation is a *false* guide, then what is to be our *true* guide? The Lord Himself is our guide. Our guidance and correction come from *God*, as we walk in fellowship with Him. In the context of loving relationship, God's Word and His Spirit guide and correct us. God also places *people* in our lives who can give us wise counsel, speaking into our lives and bringing input and correction as needed.

But we can make the mistake of allowing ourselves to be guided instead by condemnation. Why? Because condemnation seems so reasonable to us. But as a false guide, condemnation actually keeps us from receiving from the *Lord*, who is our *true* guide. When under condemnation, we keep ourselves at a distance from God. At such times, we cannot receive the *Lord's* input and correction, and we certainly cannot receive the empowerment needed to walk in victory.

God's holiness and purity, along with His love and grace, are what give us a right perspective for seeing *ourselves* clearly and evaluating our lives. God's holiness sets a standard we aspire to, and His love and grace provide an *environment* for us to grow and mature in holiness, even as we still fall short of the ultimate standard. We must learn to *see* ourselves based on how

God sees us, not based on our inevitable shortcomings. That's why Paul wants us to understand that nothing can separate us from the love of God. God wants us to evaluate our lives from the starting point of His perfect love. I'm not talking about living in denial or ignoring our sins. I'm talking about seeing ourselves based on the higher truth of our redemption. We are to see ourselves based on the work of God's *grace* in us. It's a grace that brings a *redefining* to our lives.

This is why it really does require *faith* for us to *enter into* that grace. It takes faith to enter God's perspective of who we are.

Grace is more powerful than sin.

The entire thrust of the New Covenant in Yeshua revolves around the truth that God has made *grace* available to man. Grace is more powerful than sin. That is why it's possible for you and me to experience real life transformation in spite of our flaws. Condemnation reverses that, making sin more powerful than grace in its impact on us. Never lose sight of the fact that condemnation is a lie.

LETTING GO OF REGRET

Paul gives us some helpful insight into the condemnation issue in his second letter to the congregation in Corinth. In chapter 7, he is talking about the repentance of the Corinthians in response to Paul's correction in his first letter to them. He wrote, "For godly grief produces a repentance that leads to salvation without regret, whereas worldly grief produces death" (2 Cor. 7:10, ESV).

First, let's note that Paul points out a contrast between *godly* grief over our sins and *worldly* grief. One leads to life, while the other leads to death. Let's be a little more specific because Paul does elaborate on godly grief. This *godly* grief, he says, will lead us to *repentance*. The result of true repentance is salvation *without regret*.

Repentance is what makes the difference between godly grief and worldly grief. It's worth pointing out that the Greek word for *grief* and *regret* are actually the same word. So if we translate the passage using the same *English* word in each case, it would read as follows: "For godly *regret* produces a repentance that leads to salvation *without regret...*" It almost seems like a contradiction in terms. Are we to experience regret, or not? Paul is suggesting that there is an *appropriate* regret that leads us into repentance. When we have truly *embraced* repentance, we do not have to remain in that place of regret, where we rehearse and relive our failures and shortcomings. Continuing to rehearse our regret when we have confessed and repented prevents us from moving forward in the righteousness we desire, as we continue to live under the weight of our past sins.

Clearly, it is appropriate to feel grieved when we sin. If we do not feel any grief over our sins, that indicates a hardened heart that is insensitive to God and the conviction of His Spirit. When we fall short, we are to acknowledge our sin to the Lord and ask His forgiveness. Our "godly grief" leads us to do this, but confession alone is not complete. Note the sequence Paul lays out here. Godly grief produces *repentance* in us. Remember, repentance speaks of a *turning* that takes place in our thinking and actions. Often repentance involves a *process* in which we change the way we are thinking and living, but that repentance *begins* with a resolve in our hearts to turn from sin and turn *toward God* and His ways.

Godly grief will lead us to *repentance* that "leads to salvation." Keep in mind, Paul is not referring here to what we often think of as our "initial experience" of salvation, where we first receive Yeshua and His atonement. Paul is talking about the lifelong *process* of walking in salvation. It's a process in which we continually grow in our personal experience of the saving power of the Lord. Both the Hebrew and Greek words for *salvation* point to the idea of rescue, deliverance, and wholeness. So repentance leads us into a place of wholeness and rescue from sin's ongoing power in our lives.

Then Paul writes that this is a salvation *without regret*. What does that mean? Practically speaking, I believe it means that when we have confessed and repented, we are not to rehearse our shortcomings over and over again. Sometimes we can be tempted to do this, thinking that through our repetition of how regretful we are, God will see us as being more sincere. But we are not to *live in* the place of regret. Rather, we realize that God's forgiveness brings us to a place where we can repent and truly leave our sins behind us. Lack of regret doesn't mean we *feel good* about the bad things we have done. *Of course* we feel regret over any sin or disobedience against the Lord. However, we must not keep rehearsing our failures and *reliving the grief* or disappointment we feel regarding our failures. We must let go of the regret if we want to move forward in the walk of holiness to which we are called.

> **We must let go of the regret if we want to move forward in the walk of holiness to which we are called.**

I can confess my sin, ask forgiveness, and repent from my heart. But if I continue to inwardly "beat myself up" over how bad I feel about my actions, that is *worldly sorrow* and according to Paul, it leads to death. The "death" he refers to here is not physical but our separation from the life-giving presence of God. It's not that God has rejected us from His presence, but our believing the lie of condemnation leaves us convinced that God does not desire our fellowship. In *our thinking* we are separated from God's presence, and that will surely lead to death in our spiritual lives. Persistent condemnation will actually keep us *tied to* the sin we feel so bad about. It leaves us *feeling* guilty even though Yeshua has fully paid the price for our forgiveness and freedom. We allow the sin to define us, rather than our new identity in Yeshua, unless we can *receive* forgiveness and cleansing. When our sin is the basis for how we see ourselves, we will continue in the sin rather than leave it behind by God's grace.

The truth is, God has provided an amazing salvation that frees us to live *without regret.* That means we don't have to recount our failures over and over again. Really, that is often just a form of works-righteousness. We are tempted to feel like the more we verbalize our regret, the clearer it will be to God that we are really sorry. We think that maintaining and declaring our regret makes our confession more sincere.

But repeatedly verbalizing our regret does nothing to actually relieve us of the sense of failure we feel. The more we lament over our shortcomings, rather than stepping out from condemnation, the worse we feel. Lingering regret leaves us weighed down by the sin we have already confessed to the Lord. Regret is like fuel thrown on a fire. It "feeds" our feelings of condemnation.

In writing of a salvation "without regret," Paul was likely drawing from his personal experience. In a previous chapter, we referenced a statement from 1 Corinthians 4. He wrote, "In fact, I do not even judge myself. For I know of nothing against myself, yet I am not justified by this. It is the Lord who judges me" (1 Cor. 4:3b–4). Paul understood that God alone is qualified to judge. As human beings, our own judgments are not guaranteed to be pure and righteous. Thus, we can understand why Scripture exhorts us not to be judgmental toward other people.

Paul actually takes this a step further, applying the principle to his view of himself. Paul certainly believed in the importance of regularly assessing our lives through healthy self-examination (see 2 Corinthians 13:5). But when self-examination leads us to pronounce judgment over ourselves, it goes too far. Again, God is the only One perfectly righteous and pure in His judgments; therefore, *God's* judgments are the only ones that should mean anything to us. And what has God chosen to do with the judgment we deserved for our sin? He placed it on Yeshua, forgave us, and released us from the guilt of our sins.

Condemnation is a form of pronouncing judgment over our lives. Nagging guilt, even after we have confessed our sin, is like a judgment against ourselves, leaving us condemned rather than free. What Paul is showing us in writing that he "know(s) of nothing against (him)self..." is that he puts no confidence in *human* judgments, even in relation to his own shortcomings. Yes, he was *aware* of his shortcomings, but he did not pass judgment on himself. Only God is righteous to judge, and for Paul, that translates into the declaration, "I know of nothing against myself."

He refused to give any credence to the judgment of self-condemnation, even though he had sinned greatly in his past. His own judgments against himself were not to be trusted. His own judgments neither justified nor condemned him. Condemnation is a manifestation of trusting in our own judgments against ourselves, but in fact, condemnation cannot be trusted. How liberating it is for us to fully believe this!

We must see that simple and sincere confession of our sin really does position us to fully receive God's forgiveness and cleansing. The simplicity of God's provision defies logic and natural thinking. But it *is true*, and the only way we can enter this grace is through faith.

In the next chapter, we will continue our focus on condemnation and see why the devil works so hard to keep us trapped in this counterfeit influence.

CHAPTER SIX

SEEING THE WAY GOD SEES

We must remember that God has a specific goal or *intent* with His work of grace in our lives. Seeing this intent can help us further understand the crippling nature of condemnation. We have touched on the truth of Romans 8:29—that God's ultimate goal for every believer is "to be conformed to the image of His Son…" We must remind ourselves of this powerful concept daily— that God's goal for our lives is to cause us to become truly *like* Yeshua.

This takes place in the context of growing relationship with the Lord. Unless we see that this *relationship* is key to what salvation is all about, we miss much of the *purpose* of salvation. Again, our relationship with the Lord is the context for us to grow into a likeness to Yeshua. Much can be said about this issue, but I am touching on it briefly here to provide some context for the rest of the chapter.

There is a basic principle related to human interaction—we take on similar characteristics to those we spend much time with. For example, we read in Proverbs 13:20 that "whoever *walks with* the wise *becomes* wise" (ESV, italics added). This principle is true in our relationships with other people, and it's also true in our relationship with God.

Consider how parents and children display similar personality traits and mannerisms. This does not simply reflect the *genetic* connection between parents and children; I believe it also reflects the *relational* connection. Children spend time with and *watch* their parents and often adopt similar mannerisms. This is also true in our walk with God as His beloved children. The more we spend time with God through worship, prayer, and His Word, the more we become like God, taking on characteristics of His own nature. This is part of our being created *in His image,* as Genesis 1:26 informs us. Our worship, prayer, and attention to Scripture become part of our *watching* God, so to speak.

In that context, our own life and nature are impacted. This is not something we necessarily plan out or calculate. Essentially, it *just happens* in the context of our *relationship* with Him. This is why David could write in Psalm 34 that those who *look to* the Lord are radiant. As His children, we *behold Him,* and we are affected by His beauty and glory, as we ourselves *become* radiant.

This is key to the process of our becoming *like* Yeshua and conformed into His image. The context for this supernatural work is *relationship* with the Lord. But condemnation leaves us thinking that God does not *want* relationship with us. If we believe this counterfeit influence, we will be unable to experience this glorious process of becoming like Yeshua. God's ultimate goal for our lives is nothing less than our growing likeness to His Son.

Elsewhere, Paul uses slightly different wording for describing this goal. In 2 Corinthians 3:18, he writes, "But we all, with unveiled face beholding as in a mirror the glory of the Lord, are being transformed into the same image from glory to glory—just as from the Lord, who is the Spirit." Paul is referring to the New Covenant ministry of the Spirit to cause *our* lives to be conformed to *Yeshua's* likeness, as we keep our eyes on Yeshua. We are *beholding* the Lord, or *watching* Him, and our lives are changed in the process. A *supernatural* work of the Spirit takes place when our focus is on Yeshua.

FROM GLORY *TO* GLORY

Paul uses an interesting phrase in describing this transformation process, and I think the phrase is insightful. He says our process of transformation is *"from* glory *to* glory" (italics added). I used to read this passage and feel like the phrase was somewhat mystical. What does it even mean to go from glory to glory? How is it relevant? As I prayed over this, the Lord showed me some things that are very practical to our walk. Let me explain.

When we focus on ourselves and our shortcomings, we are tempted to feel discouraged and unworthy because our lives are not yet where we want them to be. But *God sees* differently. In our times of struggle, God sees *even those times* as part of a supernatural process of advancing in His glory, as we are diligent to confess our sins and repent. The key is that, even when we have struggled, we continue to *receive* his correction, trust in His grace, and continue to keep our eyes on Yeshua as we grow in our *relationship* with Him.

If we respond to His correction with a "yes" in our hearts, we will advance in His glory.

In responding this way, we are not *denying* our struggles or pretending they don't exist. Rather, we are seeing daily, by faith, that our lives are now *in Yeshua*. This does not "compute" with our natural thinking, but it's all about how *God sees* us in Messiah. If we *respond* to His correction with a "yes" in our hearts, we will *advance* in His glory, as our lives are *being* changed *from* glory *to* glory.

Let me put this in different wording that I think can be helpful. Using natural reasoning, what would make sense to us is the idea that *advancing* involves going from *failure* to glory. But in God's thinking, we are going *from* glory *to* glory. Even though our experience involves *moments* of failing, God never *sees* us as failures. Based on heaven's thinking, we are always going from glory to glory. Why? Because God never sets aside *His vision* for us to become like Yeshua. He fully intends to finish the work He has begun in us. Yes, it's a *process,* and it continues over the course of a *lifetime.* But we can struggle with this concept of going *from* glory *to* glory because it might not fully make sense to us. Yet, in those places of our walk where

He sees us based on the destiny He has for us, not based on moments or seasons of stumbling.

we see failure, *God* sees glory because He is seeing us based on where He is taking us. He is taking us into a growing likeness to Yeshua. *That's how God sees us.* He sees us based on the destiny He has for us, not based on moments or seasons of stumbling. This is why He keeps no record of our sins—because He sees us based on *His vision* for our lives, not based on how we have fallen short of that vision.

Now, just to clarify, I am *not* saying that those times when we sin or stumble are themselves glorious. I am also *not* saying that God is just tolerant of our sin and fine with us living however we want to live. I am not saying that we should be *content* with times or seasons of compromise or disobedience in our lives. What I *am* saying is this: *God sees* us differently than we see ourselves, even when we have let Him down. In such times, He *sees us* as being in that supernatural process of going from glory to glory. This is *totally grace.*

There is nothing reasonable or logical about this. It is God's gift to us, and it will never make sense to our natural minds. What makes *more* sense to *us* is condemnation, yet *God says* we are going from glory to glory as we respond to times of stumbling by acknowledging our sin, repenting, and renewing our pursuit of relationship with Him. *Grace* is what makes this possible.

Over the years, I have heard dozens of "definitions" of grace. One such definition I truly love is this: *Grace is the empow-*

ering work of God, enabling me to *become* the person God *already* sees me as being. God sees you and me according to the calling and destiny He has set for our lives. Based on His vision for what I am becoming, He gives grace to empower me *for* that. There are numerous examples of this principle in Scripture. Let's just look at a few of them.

GRACE FOR *BECOMING*

Abraham was the first patriarch of Israel and the spiritual father of all followers of Yeshua—Jew and Gentile alike. Abraham and his wife, Sarah, were childless and had reached the age at which having children was not possible. Abraham's original name had been Abram, but in Genesis 17:5, God *changes his name* to *Abraham*, which means "a father of multitudes." God tells him, "No longer shall your name be called Abram, but your name shall be Abraham; for I have made you a father of many nations" (NKJV).

Changing his *name* was significant. In our modern culture a name is often little more than a means for identifying a person. We might give a child a particular name because we like how it sounds, or because it may honor someone we esteem. But in biblical times, a name meant much more. It was almost like a prophetic declaration over the person, bringing definition and purpose to his or her life.

God *changed* Abram's name to Abraham, prophetically declaring over him his purpose and calling. Naturally speaking, there was no possibility of Abraham and Sarah having a child. But God had given the promise, and this was their destiny. In changing the name, in essence, God was changing Abram's sense of *identity*, desiring him to *see himself* as a father of multitudes. Why was this necessary? Because God had a *supernatural* calling for Abraham, and Abraham's own faith was key for him to come into this miraculous calling. God has a calling and destiny for each of our lives. He is looking for us to "partner" with Him through our faith, trust, and obedience.

God wanted Abraham to see his life in the same way *God Himself* saw him. In Romans 4, Paul refers back to Genesis

17:5, as he describes the *faith* of Abraham to *trust* in God and in the work of grace God had promised. Paul refers to Him as the God "who gives life to the dead and calls into existence that which does not exist" (v. 17). This is what God was doing with Abraham. He was calling Abraham's fatherhood into existence, even though it was impossible for Abraham and Sarah to have children, according to their human nature.

We must see a key point here: God wanted Abraham to come *into agreement* with His vision for Abraham's life, even though it made no sense. God called that which did not exist as if it did exist. This is how God sees. It's different from what logic and reason tell us. It's different from how *we* see if we are ruled by logic and reason alone, rather than faith and vision.

If we will see ourselves according to faith, the way God sees us, and leave behind the counterfeit influence of condemnation, we can move forward into a destiny that defies logic and reason.

Abraham's story should be an encouragement to us. As we observe his history we can see how flawed Abraham truly was, but that did not change God's vision and destiny for his life. This is one of the best-known accounts in the entire Bible, yet we can fail to see the practical application to our own lives. Every one of us can see logical reasons we should be disqualified from any meaningful calling in God. If we will see ourselves according to faith, the way God sees us, and leave behind the counterfeit influence of condemnation, we can move forward into a destiny that *defies* logic and reason. Our lives can honor and glorify God, in spite of those times when our obedience, trust, and even our faith, has wavered. He gives us grace for *becoming* what He has called us to be.

A couple of other helpful examples come to mind. In Judges, chapters 6–8, we see the account of Gideon, who was powerfully used by God to lead Israel to freedom from Midianite oppression. He also tore down the altar Israel had built to Baal and the Asherah pole being used to worship the false

SEEING THE WAY GOD SEES

gods of the nations. But Gideon was an unlikely hero. When the Angel of the Lord first comes to him, he is in hiding, for fear of the Midianites. Furthermore, when the Angel tells him that God is with him, Gideon expresses both skepticism and fear. He was saying, in essence, "If God is with us, why are we having all these problems?"

But what is interesting to see here is the Angel's initial greeting to Gideon. He says, "Adonai is with you, O mighty man of valor" (Judg. 6:12). That is when Gideon expresses his own disillusionment about the Lord. He is in fear and unbelief, yet the Lord *calls* him "mighty man of valor." How can this be? Again, it demonstrates the truth that God sees us according to calling and destiny. He sees us according to what is in *His own heart* for our lives. God had a calling for Gideon that would require faith, boldness, and courage. He saw Gideon and spoke to him according to that calling. At that point, Gideon was neither faith-filled nor courageous, but God looked past the unbelief and fear and called forth the man of God Gideon was destined to become. I think we could say here that, once again, God called that which did not exist as though it did, and over time, Gideon *did* come to a place of faith and courage.

PETER'S BETRAYAL AND REPENTANCE

Where else can we see this principle? The life of Simon Peter, one of Yeshua's original twelve disciples, provides us with an encouraging glimpse into God's heart. Peter, of course, is known for being quick to speak out but sometimes lacking in wisdom. The incident for which he is perhaps most infamous is his denial of Yeshua. All four of the accounts of Yeshua's life and ministry show the Lord telling Peter that he would later deny Yeshua three times. Peter was adamant in his insistence that such a thing could never happen.

However, in Luke's account, we can see interaction, not included elsewhere in Scripture. Yeshua says to him, "Simon, Simon! Indeed satan has demanded to sift you all like wheat. But I have prayed for you, Simon, that your faith will not fail. And when you have turned back, strengthen your brothers"

(Luke 22:3–4). Peter responds by declaring his unwavering allegiance to Yeshua and his readiness to die for Him if necessary. But Yeshua tells Peter that he would indeed deny even knowing Yeshua three different times. We know the story. On that fateful day when Yeshua was arrested, accused, and condemned to death, Peter does deny knowing Him.

Here is the point I want us to see. Yeshua tells Peter what will happen, and Peter *disagrees* with the Lord and denies the possibility of betrayal. But Yeshua also tells Peter that he would ultimately repent and come back to strengthen the rest of the disciples. This is an amazing thing for Yeshua to say, especially if we consider the likely emotional dynamics of the situation. Peter had been one of Yeshua's closest friends, and Yeshua *knew* Peter would betray Him and deny knowing Him.

Betrayal is certainly one of the most difficult and painful experiences to walk through. Though we know Yeshua did not sin at any time, He still *experienced the pain* of rejection and betrayal. He listened as Peter pridefully boasted of his loyalty. Yeshua knew the horror of what He was about to go through, that He would be crucified for the sins of the world. Amid this interaction that must have been filled with emotional turmoil, Yeshua's focus was on *interceding* for Peter so that his faith would not falter after his denial of the Lord.

Yeshua was looking *beyond* the pain of betrayal, torture, and death, interceding for Peter to *become* the victorious man of God he was destined to become. He tells Peter that he would indeed return to his brothers and become a rock of strength and encouragement to them. The point we must see is this. God does not just *know* our destiny; He actually *sees* us *according* to our destiny. He even intercedes for us to come into that destiny. God *sees* us for who we are *becoming*, by His grace.

If ever there was a time that it might have seemed appropriate for Yeshua to shake His head in disgust over human weakness, it was here in this interaction with Peter. But of course, God *sees differently* from how we see. Yeshua was *seeing* Peter for the man of God he was destined to become. He was neither seeing nor accusing Peter for the cowardice and unbelief he was about to display. He was not seeing him for the terrible sin he was about to commit in denying Yeshua. God *sees beyond* our times of weakness. He *sees beyond* our struggles and views us for what we are *becoming* by His grace.

Here is an amazing truth for us to recognize in this encounter: Yeshua *believed* in Peter and his calling, in spite of the pride and cowardice that would be evident in the hours that would follow. I believe Yeshua wanted Peter himself to *recognize* Yeshua's belief in him, and His words here in Luke's account express that very thing. I suspect Peter would forever remember those words: "I have prayed for you...that your faith would not fail. And when you have turned back, strengthen your brothers." It's as if Yeshua was saying to him, "Peter, I'm already seeing beyond your failure, envisioning you for the man of God you are destined to become." Yeshua's words to Simon Peter represent a powerful expression of forgiveness and grace, assuring Peter that condemnation was to have no place in his life.

At this point, you might still be tempted to dismiss these principles of grace as they relate to you personally. After all, how could God ever see *me* in the same way He saw people like Abraham, Gideon, and Peter?

Well, consider the words of the prophet Jeremiah, spoken to the *entire nation* of Judah: "'For I know the plans that I have in mind for you,' declares Adonai, 'plans for shalom (peace) and not calamity—to give you a future and a hope'" (Jer. 29:11). These words were spoken when the southern kingdom of Judah was about to go into exile for seventy years in Babylon. This was the judgment of God, necessary because of their rebellion, but God Himself never lost sight of the "future and hope" He had in mind for them.

The same is true for you and me, in spite of our shortcomings. Condemnation tries to convince us there could not be any future or hope for us. But remember that condemnation is often our way of punishing ourselves for how we have let God down. We must realize that *God* sees us for who we are *becoming*, not for how we have fallen short. Remember, condemnation is a direct attack against God's vision for our lives, declaring our destiny to be a lie. But it's condemnation that is the lie.

DO NOT LOSE HEART

When we see our shortcomings, it can be tempting to get frustrated with ourselves, and even to lose heart. Actually, there is nothing wrong with being frustrated with our shortcomings, as long as the frustration does not blind us to what we are *becoming* by God's grace. Condemnation does indeed blind us to God's vision for our lives. Paul's words to the congregation in Corinth should encourage us in this regard. He wrote, "For this reason, since we have this ministry, just as we have received mercy, we do *not lose heart*" (2 Cor. 4:1, italics added). Let's consider this verse in context to see its importance.

This immediately follows the verse considered earlier from 2 Corinthians 3:18. Understand that the chapter divisions in our modern translations were not part of the original manuscripts. My opinion is that the insertion of a chapter division between 3:18 and 4:1 can leave us missing the actual connection of these two verses. I do not believe Paul is beginning a new thought in chapter 4:1, and I think this becomes clear as we note the progression of his thinking here.

In 2 Corinthians 3:18, Paul writes of the transforming of our lives "from glory to glory." He identifies this work as a ministry of the Spirit of God. As our eyes are on Yeshua, we are being transformed into His image *by the Spirit*. So, chapter 4:1 *continues* the same thought. We know this because of the word "therefore," or "for this reason" at the beginning of verse 1. He then writes, "Since we have *this ministry...*" (italics added). What *ministry* is he referring to? It does not really fit the context to say he is speaking of his own apostolic ministry to the nations. I believe he is referring to the ministry of the *Spirit* described in the previous verse. He is talking about the ministry of the Holy Spirit *to us*, to transform us from glory to glory. In God's mercy He releases this work of His Spirit to bring transformation to our lives. *Because* of this ministry by God's mercy we *do not lose hope*.

When we *want* to serve God but fall short in different ways we are *tempted* to lose heart, wondering if we are just fighting a losing battle in our desire for obedience and victory over sin. But Paul is pointing us to the *mercy* of God to *forgive* us when we fall short. Then, beyond that, there is the *ministry* of the Spirit to work transformation in us, taking us from glory to glory, even though we still fall short. Because we *have this ministry*, we do not lose heart. Yes, we can be *tempted* to lose heart, but we do not give in to it. We do not get bogged down in condemnation, as we *see* that God is indeed taking our lives from glory to glory. That is His *grace* to us, ministered by the Holy Spirit.

The thought continues in verse 2: "Instead, we renounced the hidden shameful ways..." What is his point? His point is that we *repent and renounce* shameful actions and ways, rather than allowing guilt and condemnation to prevail. In repentance, we are not denying the shameful nature of certain actions. Rather, we are acknowledging it, but then *turning* from those ways to the ways of the Lord. Instead of losing heart when we have sinned, we fix our eyes on the mercy of God, as we repent and renounce those actions that have the potential to leave us feeling shame and losing heart.

Condemnation blinds *us* to the very things *God Himself sees* in us. It blinds us to our *identity* in Messiah, and it blinds us to the *destiny* that is *rooted in* our new identity. Condemnation keeps us from seeing what we are becoming by God's grace.

THE MINISTRY OF THE SPIRIT

Paul's words from 2 Corinthians 3 can give us further insight that I think can be helpful for seeing this issue. In the quote below, I have omitted some verses in order to highlight an aspect of Paul's flow of thinking here:

> (God) who also made us sufficient as ministers of the *new covenant*, not of the letter but *of the Spirit*; for the

letter kills, but the Spirit gives life (2 Corinthians 3:6, NKJV, italics added).

For if the *ministry of condemnation* had glory, the *ministry of righteousness* exceeds much more in glory (2 Corinthians 3:9, NKJV, italics added).

But even to this day, when Moses is read, a veil lies on their heart. Nevertheless, when one turns to the Lord, the veil is taken away. Now the Lord is the Spirit; and where the Spirit of the Lord is, there is liberty. But we all, with unveiled face, beholding as in a mirror the glory of the Lord, are being transformed into the same image from glory to glory, just as by the Spirit of the Lord (2 Corinthians 3:15–18, NKJV, italics added).

This passage is rich in substance and I think there are multiple levels of meaning and interpretation. My thoughts here touch on one such level. Keep in mind, Paul is highlighting a contrast between the "ministry" of the New Covenant and what he calls the "ministry of condemnation." He is referring to the condemnation we come under when trying to follow the "letter" of God's *Torah* but do so in the power of our own natural ability. In spite of our best intentions and efforts we will inevitably fall short, and the result will be condemnation. Thus, he refers to the Law as having a *"ministry* of condemnation." In spite of the beauty and "glory" of God's *Torah*—His ways and instruction—the Law leaves us guilty and condemned, as we find we are unable to keep it perfectly.

However, through Yeshua, we have come into a New Covenant, which brings a glorious and *life-giving* "ministry of righteousness." The contrast is seen in these two statements: "the letter kills" and "the Spirit gives life."

Remember, the goal is for God's righteousness to impact our lives. The Law cannot accomplish this in us, but the *Spirit can* accomplish it. This takes place on two levels. First, in receiving Yeshua we come into a *positional* righteousness based on our faith identification with Him. Trusting in Him and not ourselves—His righteousness, not our best efforts—we receive Yeshua's righteous standing with God as a gift (see 2 Corinthians 5:21). There is also an *ongoing* work of righteousness, and this ongoing work is part of the Spirit's *ministry* to our lives, as we walk in relationship with Him. Too often, our own focus is on ourselves and our performance. *Self*-focus results in a "veil," so to speak, hindering us from seeing this glorious *ministry of righteousness* in our lives. However, when "the veil is taken away," God gives us a glimpse into what it is the *Spirit* is doing in us. The Spirit enables *us* to see what *God is already* seeing in us.

> **We must get our eyes off our failures and turn our attention to the Lord.**

What is the key? We must get our eyes off our failures and turn our attention to the Lord. We get our focus away from the ways we have fallen short, and we focus instead on the ministry of the Spirit in us. Only when looking to Him will the "veil" be removed. In context here, turning to the Lord is, specifically, turning to the Spirit, where we find liberty from the condemnation that comes from self-focus. The Spirit brings us freedom to see more clearly what we are becoming by God's grace. The Spirit enables us to see ourselves the way God sees us. Again, the Law cannot accomplish this. It cannot reveal to us what we are becoming in Yeshua. By itself, the Law shows us the high standards of God that we fail to perfectly walk in. In other words, the Law reveals to us the painful reality that we are *not righteous*.

But again, when we turn to the Lord (the Spirit), "the veil is taken away." The Spirit brings freedom from the limitations of only seeing what we are *not*, so that we are able to see, by faith, who *we are* by God's grace. Paul describes us as going "from glory to glory." To see this, we desperately need the liberty that comes from the Spirit.

The enemy's goal is to cripple us in our "seeing." As he distorts our image of who we truly are in God, he can keep us from seeing what we are becoming in Messiah. As long as the "veil" remains we will mostly see our shortcomings, and have little vision for our *transformed* lives. By turning to the Spirit and receiving His ministry, we see who we are becoming as we "behold" *His glory* and, by faith, step into the process of life transformation. This is the glorious ministry of righteousness, the ministry of the New Covenant.

As we focus on *Him* and not ourselves God's grace empowers us to become *like Yeshua*. By the Spirit, our lives participate in the grace of this supernatural "glory to glory" process.

CONVICTION IS ESSENTIAL

So, God sees us for what we are becoming. I am emphasizing this point repeatedly because it is challenging for us to see *ourselves* that way. Yet this is a key aspect of God's grace working in us. Seeing this principle can lead us to a clearer understanding of the place of *conviction* in our lives. The Holy Spirit convicts us for sin or compromise. However, we must not make the mistake of confusing *conviction* with *condemnation*. While condemnation is deadly to our spiritual life, conviction is essential to a healthy walk with God.

The point to keep in mind when we are processing the Spirit's conviction is that God wants us to keep our focus on what we are *becoming*, even as we *deal* with areas of our life the Spirit is showing us.

We all sin and fall short of the glory of God's righteous ways. We all are tempted with areas of sin, and we sometimes embrace compromise, both knowingly and unknowingly. Either way, God will bring *conviction* to help us see things in our lives that must change. God's Spirit shines His light on sin or compromise to show us ways in which our lives are not properly aligned with God's heart and His ways. Conviction is actually God's *grace* to us. He is getting our attention so we will not continue on a path that is detrimental to our walk with Him. He gets our attention through the inward prompting of the Holy Spirit, through the truth of His Word, or through the godly input of other believers in our lives. How we *respond* to that conviction is crucial.

Here is what we must see—when the Spirit is showing us something in our lives that needs to change, the issue is not how *bad we* are for *needing* to change, the issue is how *glorious the calling* is that we are falling short of.

So with conviction, God intends for us to have a sense of *hope*. He is showing us where He wants to bring us into *greater victory*. That is what conviction is truly *about*. It opens our eyes to the potential for greater victory, as we see areas where our lives can come more fully under His lordship. The key here is *lordship*. If we just want to do "our own thing," conviction does not encourage us. But when we truly desire that Yeshua is Lord over every area of our lives, conviction brings hope and encouragement.

> *Conviction opens our eyes to the potential for greater victory, as we see areas where our lives can come more fully under His lordship.*

CONVICTION AND GRACE WORK TOGETHER

We are hopeful and encouraged because God always gives us grace *along with* conviction. Conviction and grace work *together* for seeing our likeness to Yeshua develop. How are we to understand this seeming paradox? Here is what we must see. Grace will *never water down* God's conviction or leave us feeling comfortable with compromise. However, when we are convicted, grace *meets* us in our place of weakness and need, propelling us *forward* when we *embrace* God's conviction. Grace does not let us "off the hook" from *responding* to conviction with repentance and change. Actually, grace *takes away our excuses* for *not* responding.

You see, in giving us grace God forgives us and "wipes the slate clean," so to speak, as we repent of sin or compromise. Then, by His grace, we are *empowered* to start fresh and move forward more fully into the life of obedience into which conviction draws us. We *embrace* God's high standards and look to Him for empowerment to walk it out. Neither past failures nor present weaknesses have the power to hold us back, as long as our trust and focus are in the Lord and His work in our lives. *Because of grace* we have no excuse for not moving forward in victory. God's *righteous ways* are our inheritance, and grace makes this possible.

MY FIRST EXPERIENCE WITH CONVICTION

I can recall my own experience of conviction when I was a brand-new believer. To give some background, I had been drawn to the Lord through the testimony of a friend who came to faith when we were roommates in college. He was Jewish and had come to believe in Yeshua. His life changed dramatically, but at the time I was not interested in anything having to do with "religion." I just wanted to party my way through life and get high as often as possible.

Eventually, we went our separate ways, but after some time, I began to feel frustrated with where my life was going. I had a thought to contact my "religious" friend, since he seemed to have found some answers. We talked and he gave me some materials to read. About a month into my "studies," I came to three key conclusions: I now believed God was real, that He had inspired the Bible, and that Jesus was the Messiah. The only problem was, my friend had moved away, and I did not know what to do with my conclusions. But a book he gave me ended with a sample prayer for receiving Yeshua as Messiah, so it made sense to me to pray the prayer in the back of the book.

So now, as a Jewish young man, I found myself believing in Jesus, but still I did not know what I should do. I had never attended a church in my life, so it didn't occur to me to do that or to contact anyone. Who would I contact? I didn't know any other believers. I did pray a little and did some Bible reading, but beyond that I had no concept of what it means to walk with the Lord. I knew there was something different happening in my life, but without the fellowship of other believers, I was clueless as to what was happening or what I should do.

After about a month, I received a call from another friend I had not heard from since college. Apparently, my Jewish friend alerted him to follow up on me. He and his wife, who had become believers after our college days, invited me to join them for a Friday-night service at a "Messianic congregation" in our area. I remember thinking to myself, "maybe the people at this congregation believe what I believe now," so I gladly joined them for that service.

The concept of Jews believing in Jesus was new to me, even though I did realize Jesus was a Jew. I had no idea that such a thing as a Messianic synagogue even existed, but I was glad to check it out. Throughout the service I was drawn to the joy of the worship, as well as the familiarity of the Hebrew liturgy. I felt the presence of God, though I had no understanding of it as such. The concluding portion of the service was the message shared by the rabbi of the congregation. That is when my world was turned upside down.

The message had to do with living our lives fully committed to the Lord. As the rabbi shared, I felt my whole life was being challenged, but in a good way. It was not what I would consider a "heavy" message, yet hearing God's Word preached, I felt my own sin being exposed to me. It was not just individual sins, but I felt my lifestyle and basic values were being challenged. I had been living my life based on *my own* ways and preferences. The deception of my self-serving ways was being unmasked. As I sat through the message, I knew that the only acceptable response to what I was hearing was to completely alter my life's direction.

On one hand, I can recall the feeling of *discomfort* as I began to consider obvious areas of my lifestyle that would have to change. In a strange way, that I did not understand, having the sin of my life exposed *felt so good*. Of course, the reason it "felt good," to put it in terms of feelings, is that it was God Himself who was stirring my heart. When the Holy Spirit convicts us of sin, He is actually stirring our hearts, connecting with us Spirit to spirit. He is giving us a sense that there is something much better for our lives, but it is hindered by the sin or compromise that is in the way.

With conviction there is an inward *knowing* in our spirit that God is doing something good. We are getting a small glimpse of the fact that God is offering us something better than what we have been settling for.

Holy Spirit conviction has two key dimensions:

1. First, God's Spirit identifies some area(s) of life in which God is showing us our need to change.
2. Also, conviction stirs within us a sense of vision and hope for a higher life of freedom and purity—a life we truly long for deep in our hearts.

In my case, I didn't *understand* what was happening; I just knew what I was *feeling*. The reason conviction "feels" good is that our spirit is perceiving things that God is speaking by His Spirit. It brings about an uplifting sense of God's cleansing work in our lives.

I can recall the months after that initial service. I remember that I just couldn't get enough of services and meetings. I relished every opportunity to be where God's Word was preached. I especially remember always *hoping* the message would be *convicting*. I did not yet understand it, but I knew that when I felt conviction, I felt uplifted. Whenever my life was being challenged, I knew that God was showing me, not just what was wrong, but a greater *freedom* He was offering to me. My life had been weighed down for twenty-five years with much sin and rebellion, but God's conviction helped me identify the sins, ministering to my heart a sense of *hope* for continuing to grow in freedom. I had no biblical understanding yet at that point, but through the goodness of God, I was able to receive His conviction as His *grace* to my life, not as His condemnation.

OBSTACLES TO WHAT WE ARE BECOMING

God does not show us our faults to condemn us. He is not looking to shame us. Rather, He is showing us things that are obstacles to what we are becoming. He wants *us* to see it for ourselves and not settle for less. The question is, will we say "yes" to God from our hearts? God fully knows we are not yet capable of a perfectly righteous life. But we *are* capable of *loyal hearts* that love and desire God above all else, even though we still fall short. That is what God is looking for in us. He is looking for the heart response that says "yes" to His lordship in our lives, even though we walk it out imperfectly.

This shows us the key difference between condemnation and conviction. Condemnation leaves me guilty and condemned when my performance is lacking. Condemnation leaves me feeling hopeless and filled with shame, as I remain focused on my sin or failure. But conviction is meant to leave me *encouraged*, as I realize that God has something better for me, in spite of my present stumbling.

> *Conviction leads me deeper into my destiny in God, while condemnation prevents me from even seeing my destiny in God.*

Conviction leaves me encouraged, as I remind myself that God *is advancing* my life from glory to glory, as I embrace and take part in this amazing supernatural process of life transformation. It's a process that includes *recognizing* my sin, confessing, and repenting—all to get me back on track. Conviction is not meant to leave me in the pit of condemnation. Conviction leads me deeper *into* my destiny in God, while condemnation prevents me from even *seeing* my destiny in God.

REVISITING ROMANS 8

In the previous chapter, I indicated that I had been struck by the fact that Paul begins and ends the powerful chapter of Romans 8 with strong statements about our freedom from condemnation. What was his reasoning behind this? We can only speculate, but my sense is that Paul was being quite intentional in ordering the chapter in this way. Of all Paul's writings, Romans 8 is his most comprehensive description on the work and ministry of the Holy Spirit in the life of the believer. So he begins the chapter with the definitive declaration that now, there *is no condemnation* for those who are in Messiah. This is to be the new *starting point* for the believer. It's a new lens through which we are to see our lives. There is *no condemnation*.

Remember, condemnation is a counterfeit influence the enemy uses to deceive us into thinking that *God Himself* sees us as guilty and condemned. This is why Paul's statement at the close of Romans 8 is emphatic in declaring, "Who shall bring a charge against God's elect? It is God who justifies. Who is the one who condemns? It is Messiah, who died, and moreover was raised…and who also intercedes for us" (Rom. 8:33–34). Yeshua, the righteous and sinless Son of God, gave Himself to die for our sins. *That's why* there is no condemnation.

So Paul begins and ends the chapter with these strong declarations of our freedom from condemnation. I believe he does this to make the simple point that the walk in the Spirit described throughout Romans 8 becomes impossible as long as we allow any place for condemnation in our lives. That's how destructive it is. If we give our attention to the false guide of condemnation, we cannot live the life in the Spirit that is available to us. Paul *begins* the chapter by stating our freedom from condemnation, and then he *ends* the chapter by *restating* our freedom, along with the reasons why we can be *confident* in this freedom. Life in the Spirit, which is essential for our own spiritual growth, will never be possible for those who live under the burden of condemnation.

What we are talking about here is not just a superficial ignoring of sin, leading to a "cheap" grace. Rather, it's a realization that the power of God's *grace* is as awesome as the beauty of His *holiness*. God does not reveal His holiness to frustrate us with an impossible goal. Rather, He is giving us vision for what our own lives are becoming.

There is another point that is interesting to note at the end of Romans 8. Paul asks the question, "Who shall separate us from the love of Messiah?" He mentions different things and makes it clear that nothing of this world has the ultimate power to separate us from God's love. Note that everything he cites is something outside ourselves. His conclusion is that nothing we encounter in this life has the power to separate us from the love of God.

The one thing Paul does not say is that *we* cannot separate *ourselves* from God's love. You see, ultimately, you and I *do* have the power to keep ourselves separated from God's love, and condemnation is one of the main ways we do this. No, God *never* stops loving us, but we can separate *ourselves* from His love when our unworthiness is more believable to us than His grace. Remember, *unworthiness* is based on what makes sense to us, while *grace* is an unreasonable gift. We must keep that in mind as we process these issues from day to day.

GUILT *AND* SHAME REMOVED

For many believers, the enemy uses *shame* to try to convince us that we are unlovable. For some folks, shame can be a result of ways we have been *sinned against*, but it also comes as we struggle with the seriousness of our *own* sins. In Yeshua our guilt *and* shame have been taken away.

Why do I mention guilt and shame separately? Aren't these just different words for describing the same thing? No, I believe there is a difference. Sometimes people will acknowledge their belief in God's *forgiveness*, while struggling to shake the sense of *shame* they still feel for their sins. Shame is something that goes deeper than just a guilty conscience. It weighs on our thoughts and emotions and often leaves us feeling worthless, seeing little or no value to our lives.

As I have been emphasizing, God attributes *great* value to us, wanting to take us from glory to glory, but shame prevents us from seeing and embracing this truth. Two different Hebrew words are translated as "glory," and Paul would have certainly been familiar with both words. One is *kavod*, and the other is *tiferet*. *Kavod* speaks of the weightiness of God's glory presence, while *tiferet* conveys the idea of beauty, splendor, and value. Paul may have had both concepts in mind when writing of our transformation from glory to glory.

The Greek word for glory in 2 Corinthians 3:18 is *doxa*, suggesting a *dignity* that is involved in this glory-to-glory process. So, putting these thoughts together, *glory* speaks of weightiness, beauty, value, and dignity. The idea of our transformation from glory to glory is related to the sense of value, beauty, and dignity *imparted* to our lives in relationship with Yeshua. While this is more clearly stated and defined in the New Covenant, it is not a new concept, in my opinion. I believe we get a glimpse of this in God's relationship with Israel, as described in the Hebrew Scriptures.

Consider what is referred to as the Aaronic, or priestly blessing, from Numbers 6. It was given to Moses shortly after Israel had been freed from slavery in Egypt. God instructed Moses concerning the declaration of the blessing over the people:

> Speak to Aaron and to his sons saying: Thus you are to bless *Bnei-Yisrael* (the sons or children of Israel), by saying to them: '*Adonai* bless you and keep you! *Adonai* make His face to shine on you and be gracious to you! *Adonai* turn His face toward you and grant you *shalom* (peace)!' In this way they are to place My Name over *Bnei-Yisrael*, and so I will bless them (Numbers 6:23–27).

This blessing is repeated in every synagogue worldwide as a part of every Jewish service. It is regarded as a "traditional" benediction, but we must see that God intended so much more than tradition alone here. Central to the blessing is the idea of God graciously *imparting* His empowering presence to the people. God's *face* was to be turned toward the people and *shine* on them for imparting His grace and peace. The Hebrew word for "His face" is *panav,* which is also translated "His *presence.*" The impact of God's face or presence turning toward the people and shining on them was that God's *name* was placed over them. The name reveals one's *identity,* and in this case, it is the identity of *God Himself.* This was being *imparted* to Israel every time the blessing was proclaimed.

For Israel, relationship with God was to be the basis for her very *identity.* God's *face shining* on her was meant to impart a very real sense of His presence. I believe God's intent here was that Israel herself would *see* who she truly is as a chosen nation in loving relationship with God. After having been freed from slavery in Egypt, she would gain a whole new identity and sense of value from her relationship with the Lord. God's face shining on her was to have a defining impact, just as *we* can behold *Yeshua* face to face and be transformed into His likeness.

I realize that Israel's experience of relationship with God was not identical to what is available to us in the New Covenant. Israel's relationship points us prophetically to a greater relationship that is possible through faith in Yeshua. I believe King David had a glimpse of this truth, expressed in his words from Psalm 34:6: "They who *looked to Him* were *radiant*, and their faces will *never be ashamed*" (italics added).

We see here the principle of God's face shining on the people and imparting His own beauty and radiance. This is the impact of salvation. Isaiah 61 describes this impact powerfully. Keep in mind that in Luke 4:14–21, Yeshua cited this passage as one speaking of His own ministry to "proclaim the year of Adonai's favor...to comfort all who mourn...to give them beauty for ashes, the oil of joy for mourning..." (Isa. 61:2–3). Isaiah then writes in verse 7, "Instead of your shame, double portion. Instead of disgrace, they will sing for joy..." Both this passage and Psalm 34:6 picture God's glory and beauty as a *contrast* to shame. God exchanges our shame for His glory, and the context for this is relationship.

God exchanges our shame for His glory, and the context for this is relationship.

We must be alert to the devil's attempts to influence us through shame because it will interfere with our relationship with God. When we sin, our fellowship with God is interrupted until we confess our sin and receive afresh His forgiveness and cleansing. In such times, we might "feel" guilty in relation to our sinful thoughts or actions. The enemy uses our feelings of guilt to try to lead us into a place of shame. He wants to convert our guilty *actions*, which were real, into *shame*, which is a deception. The devil, through accusation and lies, seeks to take us from seeing that we have *done* wrong to embracing shame as part of our *identity*. We must keep in mind that the Scriptures consistently portray God's glory and beauty imparted in relationship as a *contrast* to shame. Remember, our salvation in Yeshua is first and foremost a salvation of *relationship*. God imparts His glory and radiance as we look to Him, not ourselves. It's God's grace to us that makes this possible.

We have seen in several Scriptures the simple truth that God exchanges our shame for His glory. Shame leaves us feeling we have no value, but God imparts to us the limitless value of His own life and nature, making freedom and transformation possible. What makes sense to us when we have sinned is to wallow in shame, but God wants to lift us out from shame through the power of relationship. He has no interest in leaving us in shame. His interest is in transforming our lives so that we become like Him. In God's view, we are going *from* glory *to* glory. He never sees us as failures who lack value to our lives. Such is God's unreasonable grace. He provides us with a salvation in which He gives us beauty for ashes and glory for shame.

In relation to this, one last Scripture can be encouraging to consider. In Philippians 2, Paul gives us a description of the nature of Yeshua's saving work on our behalf. He writes in verse 8, "He (Yeshua) humbled Himself—becoming obedient to the point of death, *even* death on a cross" (italics added). It's interesting that Paul ends this statement with the phrase "even death on a cross." Why did he add this phrase? I suspect it was for emphasis, suggesting that the *type* of death Yeshua was submitted to gives us deeper insight into the full scope of the salvation and freedom He makes possible.

We know that Yeshua submitted to death to take away the guilt and judgment we deserve. It was a *substitutionary* death, meaning that He died in our place. We deserved death and judgment for our sins, but He took the punishment upon Himself in our place. Yeshua's death was a monumental event in salvation history, yet Paul felt the need to *add* a statement to his description of Yeshua's death so that we would have a fuller view of salvation's power. It was *even* death *on a cross*. We know crucifixion was a common form of Roman punishment in that day, but it was not just an instrument of torture; the cross was seen as a place of shame.

Here is what I believe we must understand—when Yeshua submitted to that death on the cross, He not only dealt with the legal issue of our *guilt*, but I believe we could say that He also bore our *shame*. In taking our *guilt* on Himself, Yeshua paid the price for *judgment* to be removed from us, in a legal sense.

But then, taking our *shame* on Himself, I believe He was paying the price for our shame to be removed in the realm of our emotions and identity. Thus, we are freed from the legal judgment against us, resulting in *no condemnation* for those who are in Messiah Yeshua. But we are also freed from the emotional weight that shame brings to our lives, opening the way for us to receive glory *in place of* shame, as we pursue God in relationship. On a practical level, the removal of shame frees us to embrace and pursue the "glory to glory" process in which the Lord transforms our lives.

FINAL THOUGHTS ON CONDEMNATION

For every human being who has ever lived, God's *displeasure* is a totally *reasonable* expectation. But God defies what is reasonable, giving us mercy and grace instead. One of the most liberating *faith steps* we will ever take is to step out beyond the condemnation we know we deserve, and to see our lives, instead, based on how God Himself sees us.

We must fill our hearts and minds daily with God's Word and promises, which speak to us of how God sees us. Fill your heart with the promises that speak to you about what you are *becoming* by His grace, knowing that whatever power sin has in this world, the power of God's grace is *much greater*. It's a grace that enables you to *become* the person God *already sees* you as being.

If you have committed your life to Yeshua, God Himself believes in you, just as He did with Simon Peter. He believes in the *destiny* He has for your life, and Yeshua is *praying for* you to fully come into it. There is a mighty man or mighty woman of God waiting to rise up in you, and God is calling that forth in your life. Don't let condemnation define you based on things you have done wrong. Confess your sin and turn from it, realizing that God Himself sees you based on the truth of your being a beloved son or daughter.

Remember, He is the God who "calls those things which do not exist as though they did" (Rom. 4:17, NKJV). As He looks at your life, is there anything not yet existing that God wants to call into being? I suspect that for all of us, the answer is yes. He is looking for our faith and our agreement, as we see ourselves for who we are becoming by His grace. Do not come into agreement with the enemy's narrative that God has written you off. God wants us to believe *with Him* for a life and calling that might appear unreasonable to us, based on past mistakes and where our lives may be at today. Grace makes the unreasonable a possibility, when we receive it by faith in our lives. It's time to get on track for a life that takes us from glory to glory. You can be certain that His grace is big enough to forgive you of sin, cleanse you of guilt, and empower you with His righteousness.

CHAPTER SEVEN

THE SUPERNATURAL PEACE OF GOD

Based on Romans 14:17, I am focusing on three foundational works of the Holy Spirit to impact our lives with God's grace. God imparts to us a supernatural *righteousness* we cannot earn and do not deserve, supernatural *peace* that steadies us as it guards our hearts and minds, and supernatural *joy* that inspires and energizes us. We began with the righteousness issue because it represents a doorway into every other blessing of God's grace in our lives. Receiving God's *righteousness* is related to our *standing* with God and the growing relationship we experience with Him as His children. Our righteousness is to shape our personal sense of identity and also our lifestyle and behaviors as a people representing Yeshua to the world around us.

Walking in God's *peace* and *joy* is related to our inward disposition, especially seen amid challenging circumstances and trials. As we walk through adversity and "storms" of life, our desire is for God's Kingdom to reign in our hearts. Keep in mind that God is never anxious and never discouraged. When we allow Him to rule in the inner realm of our thoughts and emotions, the result will be peace and joy, even when we are tempted with anxiety or discouragement.

God's peace and joy are not *only* for times of adversity. It's just that they are often most evident in such times. His peace and joy are actually aspects of the *Spirit's fruit* in us, and as such, we can consistently walk in this fruit by God's grace. While walking in peace and joy will obviously result in our *personal* inward blessing and well-being, it is also an important part of our testimony to the world around us. We need *grace* for the *supernatural* peace and joy that the world might take note of in us. Let's consider this as we focus first on this peace that surpasses understanding.

THE QUEST FOR PERSONAL PEACE

I believe the issue of inward *peace* is one of the most important areas of personal victory for us as believers. It is important for our own well-being, but it's also a significant aspect of the testimony we have before those who do not know the Lord.

The world around us seems to be filled with increasing levels of anxiety. People are anxious about

Peace cannot be found in anything of this world.

the present and the future. As we see political, cultural, and economic shaking worldwide, people feel understandably unsettled by the uncertainty of what the future holds. Peace seems to be the elusive goal that people *hope* they can somehow find for their lives. Sadly, those who do not know Yeshua end up looking for peace in the wrong places, but peace cannot be found in anything of this world.

However, for us as followers of Yeshua, peace is part of our *inheritance*. We must take to heart the words Yeshua spoke to His disciples in John 14:27: "Peace I leave with you, My peace I give to you; not as the world gives do I give to you. Let not your heart be troubled, neither let it be afraid" (NKJV). Yeshua was promising a peace that comes from God.

In Hebrew, the word translated as *peace* is the well-known word *shalom,* a word rich in meaning. The intent of the word goes far beyond the simple concept of freedom from anxiety. It actually speaks of an inward sense of fulfillment and wholeness. It's a peace that is utterly different from any peace that can be found in this material world in which we live. Why? Because it's a peace that comes from the presence of God Himself in our hearts and lives. We must not look for peace in places where it cannot be found. It is found only in our relationship with the Lord.

Consider the words of the prophet Isaiah: "You (God) keep in perfect peace one whose mind is stayed on You, because he trusts in You" (Isa. 26:3). It's interesting to note that the Hebrew phrase translated as "perfect peace" is *shalom shalom.* I suspect the Hebrew word is repeated for emphasis, telling us of a peace that is perfect, total, and complete. It is not of this world, so we cannot look for peace in anything rooted in this world. We might say it is an *otherworldly* peace. That is why this peace can steady us amid the most challenging circumstances, giving us victory over the anxiety and fear that can come so naturally to us.

While this peace is a part of our inheritance in Yeshua, there is something important we must recognize: the peace of God is *not automatic.* Something *is* required of us if we want to walk in God's peace. Isaiah gives us some insight here in the verse just quoted. Our minds must *focus* on the Lord Himself.

The kind of peace we are considering has nothing to do with the *absence* of conflict, adversity, or problems. In other words, our outward circumstances are not the basis for our peace. We might be tempted to think that, if only our circumstances were different, we could experience peace. Natural thinking says, "If I can just resolve *this* issue or *that* problem, I can be at peace. If I can just resolve the conflict I'm having with so-and-so, I can be at peace." That is a wrong way to think.

The issues will never go away permanently. The conflicts we experience, while not desired, are still a part of the ebb and flow of life. When one issue gets resolved, another issue arises. That is just the nature of life in this present age. Peace is not the result of an absence of natural reasons to be anxious. The reality is, we live our lives amid spiritual battle and warfare. But it's in the *midst* of spiritual warfare that we attain the peace of *God*. Don't hope for a day when there is no more battle or no more adversity. That day will not happen in this life, so we must get used to finding peace amid unresolved problems and spiritual warfare. We are called to find peace even in the storms of life.

We are called to find peace even in the storms of life.

Again, we must learn to focus our minds on the Lord Himself, and His abiding presence, *in the midst* of the pressures and conflicts of this life. I believe we could say, as well, that this peace is rooted in our embracing *Kingdom values* over and above the values of this world. Let's consider a key passage from Scripture that provides us with important insight:

> Do not be anxious about anything—but in everything, by prayer and petition with thanksgiving, let your requests be made known to God. And the shalom (peace) of God, which surpasses all understanding, will guard your hearts and your minds in Messiah Yeshua (Philippians 4:6–7).

God's peace is shown to be the goal of what Paul is writing here. The process he is describing leads to the *result* of inward peace. What is clear is that Paul is presenting peace and anxiety as opposites. As stated above, we might be tempted to think we can be at peace when there is no longer any logical reason to feel anxious. That is not what Paul is saying—his point is that God's peace can be a prevailing presence in our hearts *all the time*.

Paul saw peace as something to be experienced, regardless of problems faced or temptations to be anxious. Every one of us deals with anxious thoughts. The peace that surpasses understanding is not about the *absence* of anxious thoughts but the *prevailing* of *God's* thoughts. Paul himself exemplified this. Surely the circumstances he faced often gave him reasons to be anxious, yet he was able to experience God's overriding peace instead.

BEYOND UNDERSTANDING

In describing this peace, Paul uses a phrase that is key to experiencing it. He calls it a peace that "surpasses understanding." So, the peace is *from God*, not from our natural minds. This peace is also *beyond* our understanding. Thus, we might say it is an *unreasonable* peace because it is beyond what makes sense and beyond what our natural minds can comprehend. What this tells us is that, if we process the events of life with our *understanding alone*, we will be more susceptible to anxiety prevailing in our hearts and minds than peace.

> *The peace that surpasses understanding is not about the absence of anxious thoughts but the prevailing of God's thoughts.*

Of course, we *want* to make sense of it all. As human beings, we want so badly to *understand* the challenges of life that often leave us confused or discouraged. We go through trials and find ourselves asking the questions: "How can this be happening to me? Why are these things going on in my life? Lord, I just don't understand."

Such questions and thoughts are normal during times of struggle. But as we focus on our *lack* of understanding, we can open the door to anxiety because *God's* peace is not *found* in the realm of natural understanding—it's found in the realm of faith and trust. When we set our focus on trying to make sense of things, trying to understand, our *lack* of understanding actually can open us up to being anxious.

We must remind ourselves in such times, and determine in our hearts, that there is something *better* than understanding that can rule in our thoughts and emotions. While *we* may think, "I just need to *understand* what's going on here," *God* wants us to get our focus on that realm of His rule that is beyond our understanding because that is where *His* peace is found. When we insist on having to understand, yet find that our understanding or reasoning is not being satisfied, anxiety will prevail. God's peace does not come as a result of understanding and logic being satisfied. His peace is beyond what we can understand with our minds.

The prophet Isaiah gives us some helpful insight related to this issue. He wrote, "For as the heavens are higher than earth, so are My ways higher than your ways, and My thoughts than your thoughts" (Isa. 55:9). Think about what God is telling us here. The difference between *His* thinking and *our* thinking is as great as the gap that presently exists between heaven and earth. When we seek to *understand* everything we go through we are limiting ourselves to an earthly, or natural, level of processing.

In essence, what we are doing when we insist on understanding is trying to figure God out, but His thoughts and ways are on a whole different level from ours, so trying to figure Him out will just leave us frustrated and *not* at peace because His ways are higher than ours. That's why what *God* offers us is a peace that goes beyond the limitations of human understanding. His supernatural peace frees us inwardly from the *need* to understand. When I am inwardly at peace amid the storms of life, I am far less concerned about understanding *why* the storms are happening.

If we *require* understanding to feel at peace, we will not be *able* to fully experience the peace we seek. I am not suggesting that God will never give us understanding related to trials we go through. Sometimes He does, and it's certainly not wrong to *ask* for understanding when we are going through problems or confusing circumstances. My point is that we do not have promises in God's Word that give us an *assurance* that we will always understand. What God does promise is a *peace* that is superior to understanding.

A basic question we must embrace for our lives is this: Can we be *content* in those times when we *don't understand*? Or will we always insist on understanding before we can be at peace?

TRUSTING WITH YOUR HEART

Being content amid problems is ultimately the evidence of our *trust* for God. We read in Proverbs 3:5, "Trust in the Lord with all your heart, and do not lean on your own understanding." Our *trust* for God is not based on our ability to figure everything out. It's not based on our ability to make sense of things happening to us. Rather, trust for God is rooted in our basic heart stance of knowing that He is the sovereign Creator and Lord and that He is a faithful, loving, and good Father who will never abandon us. We choose to believe God really does know what He's doing in His leadership and oversight of our lives. We *trust* this with our *hearts*, even in times when nothing seems to make sense to our understanding.

David provides us with a powerful example of this kind of trust. In Psalm 31, he describes the "affliction," "distress," and "sorrow" he was going through at the time. His adversaries were coming against him, but so were his "acquaintances" and "neighbors." Outwardly, things were not going well for David, but he does not complain or express anxiety. Rather, he declares his *trust* for God: "But I trust in You, Adonai. I said; 'You are my God.' My times are in Your hands" (Ps. 31:15–16a).

David's simple statement of knowing his "times" were "in (God's) hands" is powerful. He trusted God from his heart, even when everything in life seemed to be going wrong. He believed his life was under the loving and sovereign oversight of God's leadership, even though people and circumstances were coming against him. Was he *tempted* with anxiety? He indicates as much, referring in verse 22 to the sense of "alarm" he felt, but he ultimately declares the goodness and love of God amid adversity. *Trusting* God, he could be at peace even when afflicted by opposition and troubles. David certainly did not walk this out perfectly, but he does stand out as an inspiring example of trust for the Lord.

We, too, must grow in the place of trusting God with all our hearts. And then, we are instructed not to "lean on" our understanding. The Hebrew word translated as "lean on" means to support one's self. As discussed earlier, we are not to look to our understanding as a support system, or something we can *lean* on, to have peace of mind. We simply cannot depend on it because it is ultimately an unreliable source of peace.

We must learn to be speaking according to faith, even when we are aware of inward uncertainty. We might be tempted with anxious thoughts, yet we want to speak in faith because we do believe God's word and promises, and we believe in His goodness and faithfulness. I suspect there are also times when we can deceive ourselves. We say we totally trust God, but inwardly anxiety seems to prevail much of the time.

If we do not find ourselves getting inward victory over anxiety, then we are *not* fully trusting Him. If this is your experience, it is not something to feel condemned about, but it's something to recognize and learn to deal with. Remember, *trusting* God is the key to *overcoming* the anxious thoughts trying to prevail in our hearts. We simply cannot lean on our own understanding. It is an unreliable support system, incapable of bringing us to a place of inward supernatural peace.

Why can we trust God even when we don't understand? Because He is totally trust-*worthy*. In the following chapter, we will consider keys for growing in our *trust* for the Lord.

CHAPTER EIGHT

SEVEN KEYS FOR WALKING IN GOD'S PEACE

At this point, you might be wondering how we can *come into* this place of trusting God more fully and experiencing His peace consistently. Let me first emphasize that the peace of God is not something we can earn. Again, we can only *receive* it. It is a gift from God, resulting from His ongoing presence in our lives.

There are seven foundational keys for growing in trust for God and experiencing His peace that surpasses understanding: relationship, love, worship, Scripture, prayer, gratitude, and forgiveness. Let's look at each of these keys in detail.

THE *RELATIONSHIP* KEY

First, we must realize that trust is not typically the result of a *moment* of decision. Yes, our will is involved in choosing to trust Him, but the trust that leads to God's peace consistently filling our hearts is something we grow into over time. Our walk of faith is a lifelong process of *growing* in our trust for the Lord. We make an initial decision to place our lives in God's hands, but real trust is something that is built up over time. How does this take place? I believe *relationship* is the major key. It's similar to the process of learning to trust *people* in our lives. Trust grows in the context of a deepening relationship.

In previous chapters, I have been emphasizing the *relationship* with God made possible by Yeshua's death and resurrection. Interestingly, the phrase Paul uses to describe the nature of this relationship is that we come into a "peace with God" (see Romans 5:1). God *makes peace* with us through Yeshua, and that peace marks the beginning of an intimate relationship with Him. As with any relationship, time and process are involved for growing in trust that brings His supernatural peace to our hearts.

We might put it this way—peace *with* God, and the relationship made possible by that peace, is what opens the way for the peace *of* God to fill our hearts and minds. Prevailing inward peace is the result of growing in trust as we walk with God in relationship. Our trust for Him is what brings to us grace for overcoming the anxious thoughts that can often seem so reasonable.

Throughout the psalms, we are given glimpses into David's sense of peace and security, in spite of the real troubles he experienced.

Again, we can see David as an example of one who lived out this principle. He begins Psalm 32 declaring the blessing of having our sins forgiven so that we might walk in relationship with the Lord. He later continues, "You are my hiding place—You will protect me from distress. You surround me with songs of deliverance" (Ps. 32:7). He is referring to the sense of safety and security he felt with God Himself as his "hiding place." David is not suggesting his life was free from troubles or distress. However, in His relationship with the Lord he found that "hiding place" where he felt secure, even in times of difficulty or opposition. Because of his *relationship* with God, he could experience peace amid troubles.

Throughout the psalms, we are given glimpses into David's sense of peace and security, in spite of the real troubles he experienced. The well-known twenty-third Psalm is a prime example. He writes, "Even though I walk through the valley of the shadow of death, I will fear no evil, for *You are with me*: Your rod and Your staff comfort me" (Ps. 23:4, italics added). Once again, we see that the darkness of David's circumstances is not what determined his outlook. The presence of God brought him peace and comfort. Knowing that God was with him, David was able to resist the grip of fear and allow God's peace to prevail over his anxious thoughts.

In John 14–16, Yeshua shares in depth with His disciples about the relationship with Him that would be possible for His followers. His focus in these chapters is the presence and work of the Holy Spirit in our lives, ministering to our hearts the reality of Yeshua's life and presence. Yeshua begins this teaching with the exhortation, "Do not let your heart be troubled" (John 14:1). After much description of the Spirit's work, He later begins to discuss the reality of the opposition His disciples would face from those who did not believe.

It is truly a work of God's grace to give us peace when we have reasons to be agitated and anxious.

He concludes the chapter with a bottom-line statement: "These things I have spoken to you, so that *in Me* you may have shalom. In the world, you will have trouble, but take heart! I have overcome the world!" (John 16:33, italics added).

Opposition and distress are certain, but for those walking with Him in *relationship*, peace is His promise amid those troubles. It is truly a work of God's grace to give us peace when we have reasons to be agitated and anxious.

THE *LOVE* KEY

The Bible has much to say to us about the *love* of God. Volumes of material have been written on this topic, and rightly so. God's love is at the heart of His reaching out to humanity to rescue us from the grip of sin and death. But God's love is not meant to be a mere *concept* that gives us information *about* Him. We are actually to be living our lives *in* His love. This is what we were created for, and it's only when we live in the realm of experiencing His love that we can be truly fulfilled, living in *shalom*. We function best in what we might call an "environment" of love. Yeshua taught His disciples about their need (and ours) for living in this realm of love. He said, "Just as the Father has loved Me, I also have loved you. *Abide in My love!*" (John 15:9, italics added). The idea from the word "abide" is to *live in* and *remain*. Because love is what we have been created for, we thrive when we live our lives in the realm of God's love.

Paul had much to say about this in his own writings. In his letter to the believers in Ephesus he shared his prayer for them that they would be "rooted and grounded in love" (Eph. 3:17). With the word "rooted," Paul is suggesting that love can be likened to *soil* in which our lives are planted, enabling us to grow and flourish. Of course, the roots of a plant draw from the richness of the soil, bringing life to the plant. The rich "soil" of God's love brings a powerful inward nourishing to our lives. "Grounded" suggests that love is like a *foundation* on which our lives are built, giving us stability.

Love is what connects us to God Himself and His presence.

Paul then expresses his prayer for us "to know the love of Messiah which surpasses knowledge, so you may be filled up with all the fullness of God" (Eph. 3:19). John expresses similar thoughts. He writes, "Now whoever *abides in love* abides in God, and God abides in him" (1 John 4:16b, italics added). What we see here is that love is what *connects* us to God Himself and His presence. Thus, when we live in that realm of God's love we are at peace. Again, this is the realm for which we were created. It is the realm in which we thrive as human beings.

This brings us back to the issue of *relationship* with God. Our daily walk with Him is the context for living in the realm of His love. A key verse to consider here is found in Paul's letter to the believers in Rome. He writes, "God's love has been poured into our hearts through the Ruach ha-Kodesh (Holy Spirit) who was given to us" (Rom. 5:5b). Every believer in Yeshua receives the Holy Spirit in our hearts.

What we see in this verse represents one of the most important aspects of the Spirit's ministry in our lives. I believe it is accurate to say that Paul is not referring to love as an idea here, but as something tangible that we can actually experience. God's Spirit imparts to us the reality of His loving presence. He *pours into* our hearts the very essence of the love of God. As we walk with the Lord day by day, communing with Him through prayer, worship, and Scripture, we can experience the Holy Spirit pouring the Father's love into our hearts. As we focus on the Lord and are conscious of the Spirit's presence and ministry, we can become aware of this "pouring out" into our hearts. We become conscious of His love in a very real way, and that love ministers deeply to our hearts.

I suspect we are *most* aware of this love when we give ourselves to focused worship, whether in a corporate gathering or privately. Because of the ministry of the Holy Spirit we can experience this uplifting impartation of the love of God on a daily basis, and it can impact us powerfully.

The problem is that sometimes we doubt the possibility of God loving *us* with this perfect love. We may assume that our failures leave us disqualified from receiving His perfect love. But the truth is, every one of us has failed God. This is why it is so essential for us to see and *believe* all that the Bible tells us about how *God sees* us. He sees us with the perfect love of a perfect Father. We can struggle with this because we do not really have a "grid" for processing such an idea. Sadly, the experience of so many with their earthly fathers has been hurtful or even abusive. Even the best of fathers are still ultimately flawed. Thus, we can struggle to comprehend the very *idea* of a Father who *loves perfectly*. But God really does see us through the eyes of perfect love. This is something for which we need the Holy Spirit's help so that we can recognize and embrace such a love.

Living in the *experience* of God's love is highly relevant to the issue of walking in God's *peace* that passes understanding. Consider another verse from John's letter, as he tells us, "There is *no fear in love*, but perfect love *drives out* fear" (1 John 4:18, italics added). God's love is a truly perfect love that has the power to drive fear from our hearts and minds. The same perfect love that drives out fear is just as powerful to drive out worry and anxiety. God loves us with a perfect, flawless love. When we walk with a consciousness of this love, fear and anxiety simply cannot remain in control. His love is more powerful, overriding the influence of fear and anxiety. I'm not suggesting that we have an "experience" of His love every moment, but we *can* have a consciousness of His love continually. Otherwise, Yeshua's words about *abiding* or *living* in God's love would be pointless. John's words about *abiding* in love would be pointless. To *live in* God's love is part of our inheritance as sons and daughters of the living God.

This world can often be a very *un*loving place—this is why the perfect love of our Father is so greatly needed. His love will never fail us or let us down. We can experience rejection and betrayal in this life and still remain unshaken because of *His* love that steadies us. This is God's *grace* to minister to our hearts in this way. Living in God's *love* is an essential key to walking in His supernatural peace that passes understanding. As we immerse our lives in His perfect love, we position ourselves to receive His perfect peace.

If this idea of *experiencing* God's love is new to you, I encourage you to ask the Lord to give you revelation of this love in your life. You might begin by searching through God's Word for all the passages of Scripture that speak of the nature and power of His love for us. Begin to meditate on these verses and declare them over your life, believing God will give you revelation of His love in a way that impacts you powerfully.

THE *WORSHIP* KEY

Experiencing God's love will inevitably lead us into a life marked by *worship*. Coming back to David, his own relationship with the Lord seems to have been somewhat unique among the different followers of God pictured in the Hebrew Scriptures, or Old Testament. I believe his walk with God is meant to give a prophetic picture of the intimacy available to *us* as followers of Yeshua and partakers of His New Covenant.

David's intimacy was rooted in the fact that worship was central to his life and values. It's in the context of worship that we can so powerfully experience the glory and encouragement of God's presence. I noted earlier from Isaiah 26:3 that God's "perfect peace" is given to the one "whose mind is stayed on You." Worship is one of the main contexts for us to keep our hearts and minds "stayed," or focused, on Him. That is the place where our trust grows and supernatural peace fills us, even in times when peace makes no sense.

David wrote, "In the multitude of my anxieties within me, Your comforts delight my soul" (Ps. 94:19, NKJV). Notice that David did not deny *experiencing* anxious thoughts; rather, God's comforts uplifted him amid his anxieties. A worship-filled relationship with God is key to the kind of peace David describes.

> *David did not deny experiencing anxious thoughts; rather, God's comforts uplifted him amid his anxieties.*

It's important to note here that when I speak of worship, I do not necessarily mean a worship *service.* A service is certainly one venue for expressing our worship, but what I'm talking about here is a *lifestyle* in which we have an ongoing flow from our own hearts to the Lord. We are not waiting for an *event* to worship God. We worship and honor Him throughout the day through prayer, meditation, adoration, awe, and wonder.

How does worship help us to be at peace? I think we can see worship as a faith action that opens our hearts to be able to sense the reality of God and His presence with greater clarity. Sensing the Lord more deeply, we receive grace for getting our focus off our problems. We might say that worship opens our spiritual eyes to the higher reality of God's presence and activity, even amid conflict, trials, mistreatment, pressures, and any other adversity we might encounter.

Thus, the psalmist wrote, "God is our refuge and strength, a very present help in trouble. Therefore we will not fear, though the earth gives way, though the mountains be moved into the heart of the sea" (Ps. 46:1–2, ESV). God is indeed *very* present as our help amid troubles. David expressed similar thoughts: "I have set the Lord *always before* me. Since He is at my right hand, I will not be shaken" (Ps. 16:8, italics added). God is always with us, but our walk of worship enables us to *truly see* that He is "always before me." Worship helps open our eyes to this liberating truth and to the reality of God's nearness. Although it may not make sense to our minds, such worship releases a grace for supernatural peace that truly is superior to our understanding.

THE *SCRIPTURE* KEY

Another aspect of our relationship with God that must be considered is God's Word, which is central to our walk with Him. When we love and value God's Word we position ourselves to experience His supernatural peace more consistently. The reason for this is simple. His Word does not simply inform our minds. There is a *spiritual dynamic* to God's Word, and as such, it has a powerful *spiritual impact* on our lives. God's Word is eternal, even as God Himself is eternal.

Consider John's description as he begins his own account of Yeshua's life and ministry: "In the beginning was the Word. The Word was with God, and the Word was God" (John 1:1). We must see that the Bible is not simply a collection of ideas *about* God—the Bible is an expression of the very life and nature of God.

Thus, when we read God's Word with faith and expectation, we are interacting with God Himself. This is so important for us to see. Otherwise, our times of reading Scripture can easily become mere routine or discipline. In my own life I set aside time each day for reading God's Word. On one hand, yes, my reading time is something I *schedule* into my day, so discipline and routine *are* involved. But my *approach* to these times gives me an expectation that God will be speaking to me through His Word. Often, before reading, I remind myself that as I read His Word, in essence, I am sitting at the feet of Yeshua, so to speak. I usually take a moment to just acknowledge this to God and thank Him for speaking to me as I sit before Him. To be honest, I don't always remember to do this. Sometimes I am in a hurry, or I might be thinking ahead to things I need to do that day. In such times, it *can be* more of a discipline. But when I am conscious of the idea of sitting at the feet of Yeshua and receiving impartation from Him, it brings a greater richness and quality to my times in His Word.

There is something else we need to see here. Even in those times when I am reading out of pure discipline, His Word still has a powerful *supernatural* quality that is at work *whenever* I give my attention to His Word. Remember Yeshua's own description of His words: "It is the Spirit who gives life…The words that I speak to you are *Spirit and they are life!*" (John 6:63, NKJV, italics added). We can be confident that whenever we give our attention to God's Word, which is Spirit and life, grace and life will be released through His words.

Consider Paul's thoughts from Romans 8: "Those who live according to the Spirit *set their minds* on the things of the Spirit. For to set the mind on the flesh is death, but to *set the mind* on the Spirit is *life and peace*" (Rom. 8:5b–6, ESV, italics added). Paul is giving us a key here for experiencing God's peace that passes understanding. What is the key? We are to *set our minds* on the "things of the Spirit." God's Word *is* Spirit and life. Thus, setting our minds on His Word is one key to setting our minds on the "things of the Spirit" and walking in His "life and peace." This involves reading, memorizing, and meditating on the Word. By *meditating*, I simply mean ponder a phrase, verse, or thought from the Bible. We repeat it in our minds, listening for the Spirit to give us insight. Meditation is clearly a biblical concept, even though it is often associated with Eastern religion or New Age practice.

When we set our minds on His Word, grace is released for powerful spiritual impact on our lives.

God's Word is the key to what Paul describes as the "renewing of your mind" (Rom. 12:2). In the process of our minds being renewed, there is a tearing down of old patterns of thinking and the establishing of new patterns based on God's Word. As our minds are renewed we will experience less inward resistance to the peace that surpasses understanding. Such peace still might not make sense to our natural reasoning, but as we consistently give ourselves to the process of allowing the Lord to renew our minds through His Word, we will experience grace for seeing beyond what makes sense.

As our minds are renewed we will experience less inward resistance to the peace that surpasses understanding.

Psalm 119 is an amazing work, extolling the Word of God for 176 verses. Repeatedly, the writer cites the challenges of enemies, as well as afflictions, but he always returns to God's Word as bringing life and peace amid those challenges. For example, we read, "Princes persecute me without a cause, but my heart stands in awe of Your word" (Ps. 119:161, NKJV).

Think about that! Amid persecution, rather than feeling overwhelmed by his trial, Paul is focused on God's Word and left in awe of the Lord. Just a few verses later, he shares a powerful summary statement: "*Great peace* have those who *love Your law*, and nothing causes them to stumble" (Ps. 119:165, NKJV, italics added).

David shares a similar idea in Psalm 56, written when he was fleeing from Saul *and* fearful of King Achish in Gath. He writes, "In God, whose word I praise, in God I trust; I shall not be afraid. What can flesh do to me?" (Ps. 56:4, ESV). Then after several verses of referring to the actions of his enemies, David repeats verse 4, word for word, to emphasize that God's Word was the focus of his attention and his trust.

Truly, God's Word brings an unreasonable peace to our hearts—a peace that passes understanding.

THE *PRAYER* KEY

Let's return to the passage in which Paul describes this extraordinary peace of God:

> Do not be anxious about anything—but in everything, *by prayer and petition* with thanksgiving, let your requests be made known to God. And the shalom (peace) of God, which surpasses all understanding, will guard your hearts and your minds in Messiah Yeshua (Philippians 4:6–7, italics added).

Here, Paul emphasizes *prayer* as the context for victory over our anxious thoughts. Of course, prayer is very much connected to our *relationship* with God. Too often we can make the mistake of seeing prayer as part of isolated times during the day when we bring to God our needs or the needs of others. But prayer, like worship, is something we can be involved in continually. In Paul's concluding instructions to the congregation in Thessalonica he exhorts the believers there to "Pray constantly" (1 Thess. 5:17) or "without ceasing" (NKJV).

How is it possible to pray continually? Again, prayer is part of our *relationship* with God, involving so much more than just asking Him for different needs to be met. On the most basic level prayer is about *conversation* with the Lord, so we can pray all the time. We can talk to Him continually throughout each day.

It's a *lifestyle* of praying "without ceasing" that releases grace for us to experience God's unreasonable peace. If we *pray* without ceasing, it becomes possible to experience *shalom* without ceasing. Consider the absolutes Paul uses in his words to the Philippians. What are we to be anxious about? *Nothing!* What are we to release to God through prayer? *Everything!* Think about this. Paul does not leave any room for exceptions here. This is an issue he obviously felt strongly about, seeing it as something necessary to embrace.

As believers, we *never* need to be anxious, and we *always* need to pray when tempted with anxious thoughts. We are to consciously *resist* such thoughts through prayer.

If you struggle to be at peace, please don't feel condemnation over this. The point is not to leave you feeling condemned but to help you see the goal that's *possible* for us all through prayerful relationship with God. Experiencing His peace involves a process of growth, but ultimately such peace really is possible, and Paul gives us a key.

As we experience difficulties and troubles, we are to *pray*. It really is that simple. So often, prayer can be our last resort, when it should be our first action. We should not see prayer as a formula that promises instant peace. But prayer is central to our walk with God, as we are learning to trust Him with our lives. In prayer, we learn to release to the Lord every detail of our lives, trusting in His care and sovereignty.

So often, prayer can be our last resort, when it should be our first action.

As we, in faith, release our lives into His loving hands through prayer we grow in our experience of supernatural peace. Don't try to figure this out or make sense of it. It *doesn't* make sense to our natural reasoning, but these are God's instructions to us. It all comes down to is this: Do we believe what Yeshua said to us about knowing God's peace amid the storms of life? He said this peace is to be found "in Me" (John 16:33). It's *not in* the world, but in Yeshua.

If we are to be anxious about nothing and commit everything to God through prayer, we must conclude that a life of *little or no* prayer will not experience the fullness of God's peace. Instead, we will find ourselves susceptible to the rule of worry, fear, and anxiety. The peace from God that "surpasses all understanding" comes to us in the context of prayer.

Again, we can turn to the words of David as he affirms this from his own experience: "My refuge is in God. Trust in Him at all times, you people. Pour out your heart in His presence. God is our refuge" (Ps. 62:8b–9). To "pour out (our) heart(s) in His presence" is another way of describing prayer. We see Him as our refuge, and we pour out our hearts to Him. In the process He brings us peace.

In Psalm 34, David writes, "I sought Adonai, and He answered me, and delivered me from all my fears" (v. 5). It's noteworthy that David does not say God delivered him from all his *problems,* but from all his *fears.* Yes, it's wonderful when God intervenes in the circumstances we are going through, but the reality is sometimes circumstances don't change right away, but what *can* change is our inward disposition. Victory over fear, when we have *reason* to fear, is among the greatest of victories we can experience. God's supernatural, unreasonable peace is key to that victory.

Even in times when our circumstances have not changed, committing our situations to the Lord brings our lives into the realm of His care and oversight, and that is where we can always be at peace. Remember, prayer is about *conversation* with God. As we converse with Him and release our cares and burdens to Him, this becomes an important process for giving voice to our *trust* for Him.

THE *GRATITUDE* KEY

As we grow in *trusting* the Lord, we will grow in our experience of His peace. Another practical key to this process is summed up in two words from the Philippians 4 passage, words that can sometimes be overlooked: "with thanksgiving." The simple act of giving thanks is central in our *expressing* trust for God. To thank Him during challenging times when it might not "make sense" to be thankful becomes a powerful expression of the fact that we really do *trust* God.

We might not understand what we are going through or why, but we trust Him. Our giving of thanks when it doesn't make sense actually has the effect of *nurturing and strengthening* our trust for Him. So our gratitude *expresses* trust, but it also *builds and strengthens* our trust.

Coming back to the passage from Philippians 4, prior to Paul's exhortation to "not be anxious about anything," is the exhortation to "Rejoice in the Lord always—again I will say, rejoice!" (v. 4). Paul felt this was important enough to repeat, so we must pay close attention. Our giving thanks amid circumstances we don't like and don't understand is one of the most powerful ways we can declare our trust for God. I think our thanksgiving can actually have the effect of *disarming* the natural drive we have to always want to *understand* everything. Giving thanks opens the way for God's peace to fill our hearts and minds.

When we give thanks, we are going *beyond* understanding, where peace can prevail. I find in my own life that when my heart and words are filled with thanksgiving there is little room remaining for worry and anxious thoughts. I'm not talking about a *moment* of thanksgiving, but a *mindset* of thanksgiving. Typically, it begins when I really don't *feel like* giving thanks or rejoicing. But that is what opens the way for a supernatural flow of God's peace to come in as I persist in this.

> *When we give thanks, we are going beyond understanding, where peace can prevail.*

Keep in mind that rejoicing is a *faith action* that *releases* joy. Rejoicing is not necessarily the *result* of *feeling* joy—it's a *faith act* that we do because we *trust God*, even when things are not going the way we would like. Rejoicing is a decision of our will. We make that decision in spite of the fact that we may not like the circumstances we are dealing with. But God is *always worthy* of our praise, and that is why we can always rejoice. Circumstances have no bearing on God's worthiness. Obviously, it's *easier* to rejoice when we are happy with our circumstances. But that does not bring us into the *supernatural* peace we have been considering.

Rejoicing, then, helps bring us into peace. It can bring a calming to our anxious hearts in those times when we are tempted to feel overwhelmed. As a faith action, rejoicing *lifts us above* the challenge, pain, or confusion of our circumstances. Then it brings to our hearts the *peace we need* for properly *responding* to whatever we are dealing with. You see, rejoicing is key to getting *our own* hearts in tune with *God's* heart. This is what we need for gaining the *wisdom* we desperately seek when going through trials.

What we *most need* amid adversity or opposition is *wisdom*, not simply understanding. And remember, *God does promise* us that wisdom. But this is something we can miss because too often, what we insist on is understanding. We might hold back from rejoicing because we don't understand—but God never promises that we will always understand what we are going through. Thankfully, though, He does promise wisdom, and He promises *grace* for walking through it, but there is no guarantee that we will understand it.

Unless we are willing to assume a posture of rejoicing, even when we don't understand, we will not fully enter into the peace of God that is *superior* to understanding.

Assuming the posture of thanksgiving opens our hearts to the *presence* of God and opens our minds to the *thoughts* of God. Remember that His thoughts are higher than ours. When our thoughts differ from His thoughts, we are the ones who need to change. Giving thanks is an important step we can take to help us bring our thinking in line with God's thinking.

Paul makes an enlightening statement in Romans 1. He describes man's rebellion against God since creation—rebellion that has led humanity deeper and deeper into spiritual darkness. First, he points out that God's power and divine nature are evident to man. Because of God's creation, man can clearly see who God is. Then Paul cites the *refusal to be thankful* as being at the heart of man's rebellion against God: "For even though they knew God, they did not glorify Him as God or give Him thanks. Instead, their thinking became futile, and their senseless hearts were made dark. Claiming to be wise, they became fools" (Rom. 1:21–22).

This is a sobering statement, describing the impact of man's unwillingness to be thankful. We end up cutting ourselves off from the light of God's wisdom, and our understanding becomes darkened. Why does this happen? It happens because thanksgiving is what opens our minds to God's thoughts, and *refusal* to give thanks cuts us off from the heart and mind of God. I believe Paul is shining light on the *spiritual blindness* that we open ourselves to when we refuse to be thankful. Thus, the desire we have to *understand* things *before* we will give God thanks will *keep from* us the wisdom God *wants* to give us, but when we assume the posture of thanksgiving, it opens our hearts to *receive* the light of His wisdom.

Our lifestyle of giving thanks then also becomes a testimony to *others* of the goodness of God, who gives us supernatural peace at times when anxiety makes more sense.

THE *FORGIVENESS* KEY

There is a final area that must be noted in relation to walking in God's supernatural peace. We must not allow *unforgiveness* to rule in our hearts. Although this particular issue is not tied to anxiety or fear, it is nevertheless essential for experiencing God's peace. This issue relates more to offenses and mistreatment we may encounter in the course of life.

Forgiveness is an issue to which I could easily devote a full chapter or even an entire book. However, my intent here is simply to highlight how our offenses steal our peace. We can be doing all the "right things" in terms of the six keys previously discussed, but then, we encounter mistreatment or some form of injustice, and we can find ourselves offended and struggling to forgive. It is impossible to walk in God's peace as long as we hold onto offense and unforgiveness.

The inability to forgive results in an inward agitation and unrest that can have a tormenting effect on us. I'm talking here about a *refusal* to forgive. We all have times when we struggle in this area. The pain we feel when wrongfully treated is real, and our flesh is quite resistant to quickly forgiving and letting the offender "off the hook." But as we process it with the Lord, He helps us come to the place of letting go of the offense and forgiving the offender. However, when we are *unwilling* to forgive and refuse to let go of the hurt or anger, it's as if a spiritual poison is released within us. Instead of allowing God's peace to *guard* our hearts and minds, we allow the enemy's poison to *darken* our hearts and minds.

Of course, a big part of the problem lies in the fact that our *assessment* of having been wronged may be *completely accurate*.

The offender might be either unaware of his or her offense or simply unwilling to acknowledge it and ask for forgiveness. In such cases, it can seem totally *reasonable* to us to remain angry and hold onto the offense. Focused on our anger, our hurt feelings, or our wounded pride, we can make allowances in our hearts for unforgiveness. What often happens is that unforgiveness becomes almost like a tool of our anger. Feeling hurt or offended, we withhold forgiveness as our way of privately disciplining the one who hurt us. It's our silent form of vengeance and retaliation. We convince ourselves that *when* the other person apologizes, we will forgive, but until then, it's our *right* to hold a grudge and remain offended.

Although this might make sense to natural thinking, it goes against the clear and consistent teaching of God's Word. The Bible shows us that our willingness to forgive those who have wronged us is crucial for the health of our own walk with the Lord. The issue is never the *other person* and whether *he or she* has recognized or acknowledged an offense. The issue is *me*, and whether I want my *own heart* to be clean from the poison of offense. Unforgiveness will defile us and rob us of peace. It's as simple as that.

It takes grace to forgive from our hearts, but this is clearly the standard Yeshua presents to us. The fact that we feel the pain of offense or mistreatment is the very reason why we *need* grace to forgive. It doesn't come naturally to us. Our inward sense of justice tells us that the offender deserves our scorn. But the higher priority must be our desire to walk in freedom and victory by God's grace.

The struggle to forgive can be better understood as we consider how Yeshua Himself presented this issue in what has come to be known as "the Lord's prayer." He said we are to pray "and forgive us our *debts* as we also have forgiven our *debtors*" (Matt. 6:12, italics added).

Notice that Yeshua used what we might call *debt language* in His reference to sin. The idea here is that when we have sinned against God, we incur a moral debt that we owe. Of course, this is a debt we cannot pay because our own righteousness falls hopelessly short of God's moral perfection. Thankfully, when Yeshua gave His life and died on the cross, He was paying the debt for humanity's sins. When we acknowledge our need and receive His gift by faith, our debt is canceled.

Sin results in a condition of indebtedness. When someone sins *against us* they incur a debt that is "owed" us. Yeshua's instructions on prayer make it clear that forgiveness is to rule in our hearts toward others. He gives no conditions here such as the repentance or apology of the other person. We are to forgive for a very simple reason—mercy is at the heart of *God's own* nature, and *we* are called to be *like* God as those being conformed into His image. We are to grow in the gracious nature of God Himself (see Luke 6:27–37).

Yeshua's teaching in Luke 6 is quite detailed and specific. In the passage, He makes the statement, "Forgive and you will be forgiven" (Luke 6:37). The word translated as "forgive" is different here from the word used in Matthew 6. Luke was interpreting Yeshua's exhortation as a call for us to actually *release* offenders from the "debt" they might owe us through their sin against us. Why is this distinction important? I believe Yeshua was giving the disciples, and us, a practical picture of what forgiveness is to "look like" when we have been wronged. It is not merely a verbal expressing of mercy. We are actually to give the offender a pardon by *canceling* his or her debt. If we simply say, "I forgive you," but we hold onto the sense that the other person still "owes" us, we are not seeing the level of forgiveness to which Yeshua calls us.

A number of years ago, the Lord put on my heart a simple idea that I believe He wanted me to embrace in this regard. He wanted me to see that I am to take the stance that "no one owes me." If someone sins against me, they do not owe me. If someone's actions toward me are disappointing to me, they do not owe me. This is easier said than done. Over the years since that time, whenever I am tempted with offense toward another, the Lord is faithful to remind me of that stance that "no one owes me." Despite the temptation to be offended, I embrace this by faith, and God has been good in giving me *grace* to forgive and truly release. I still do not walk it out perfectly, by any means, but I am committed to this as a foundational value for my life. By His grace, I am growing in Yeshua's likeness in this area.

Here is the bottom line on this: As long as we maintain that position—the status of being a victim who was wronged—we are not releasing. We can truly say we have released the other person when we stop mentally rehearsing our case for why we are right and they are wrong.

Let me make a strong statement to conclude this section. Our inability or unwillingness to forgive suggests that the fact that we have been *wronged* has a larger place in our hearts than the fact that we ourselves have been *forgiven*. In other words, the *offense* done *against* us is larger in our hearts than the *salvation* accomplished *for* us.

> *Our inability or unwillingness to forgive suggests that the fact that we have been wronged has a larger place in our hearts than the fact that we ourselves have been forgiven.*

If you struggle to forgive those who have wronged you, ask the Lord for a fresh revelation of *His* love and mercy toward you. Spend time reading and reflecting on various Scripture passages that highlight God's mercy and grace. His Word can change our hearts and transform us on the inside. By God's grace we can rise above the stumbling block of offenses and live in the place of the gracious heart of Yeshua Himself.

God has given us an incomprehensible grace we do not deserve. As we see this, we are to be changed in how we relate to others, as the knowledge and revelation of His love and goodness causes our hearts to become more tender. Going back to Yeshua's words from Luke 6, "Forgive and you will be forgiven" (v. 37).

As we *release* those who have wronged us, we ourselves experience *release from God,* by the presence and life of His Spirit. This is the liberty that is our inheritance as His children. This is essential for living in that supernatural peace of God that surpasses logic and understanding.

Chapter Nine

FIGHTING THE DAILY BATTLE

W hile God's peace is truly a supernatural work, we do have a role in strengthening that peace in our lives. Let's consider a passage from Paul's letter to the believers in Corinth:

> For the weapons of our warfare are not fleshly but powerful through God for the tearing down of strongholds. We are tearing down false arguments and every high-minded thing that exalts itself against the knowledge of God. We are taking every thought captive to the obedience of Messiah… (2 Corinthians 10:4–5).

Much has been taught on these verses, and my intent here is not to discuss the passage as a whole. I simply want to draw from Paul's emphasis on the role of the *mind* in dealing with spiritual opposition that comes against us. I am not suggesting that spiritual warfare is fought *only* in the realm of the mind. Rather, I am highlighting the mind as a central focus of the enemy's attack. Very often, the "battlefield" of our spiritual warfare is in our minds and emotions. We are assaulted daily by demonic attacks, and the target of these attacks is the inward life of our thoughts and emotions. The enemy seeks to influence us in the way we see God and the way we see ourselves. We must be alert to these attacks.

TEARING DOWN THE STRONGHOLDS

The "strongholds" cited here are related to *thoughts* that become a part of our basic mindset. Strongholds, in this context, can be likened to fortress walls, protecting ways of thinking that are false because they contradict God's truth. We are told that strongholds must be *torn down*. Paul refers to "false arguments" that exalt themselves above the truth of God's Word, exhorting us to mentally reject and tear down such arguments. Typically, false arguments will call into question God's goodness, faithfulness, or power. Or they will attack our own worthiness, suggesting that our personal weaknesses disqualify us from God's blessing or intervention. In either case, our faith suffers if we believe the false argument.

Paul then speaks of taking *thoughts* captive and bringing them into "the obedience of Messiah." What does it mean to take thoughts captive? The wording here gives us some valuable insight. First, Paul is speaking of aggressive action in dealing with thoughts that are not in line with God's Word. The idea is to bring those thoughts into *submission*. Thus, we should not just try to *ignore* thoughts of worry, fear, or anxiety, hoping they will just go away. We must see such thoughts as *intruders* in our minds.

Think about it. If burglars broke into your home, would you just ignore them? Would you allow them to freely roam through your home? Of course you would not! Yet sometimes, that is exactly what we do with unbiblical thoughts—we hope that if we ignore them they will eventually pass. But to simply try to *ignore* thoughts of fear or anxiety, or suppress the thoughts, is like allowing a burglar to freely roam through our thoughts. Fear, worry, and anxiety are seeking to *steal* our peace, and we cannot permit it.

So if burglars are in our homes, what does it actually mean to take them captive? We might attempt to overpower them ourselves, but a *more* effective way would be to alert the police because they have *authority* to disarm and *capture* the thieves. We must do the same with destructive thoughts the enemy uses to attack our faith and confidence in God. Thus, instead of allowing false arguments to "freely roam" in our minds, we *capture* those thoughts and imprison them, so to speak, bringing them into submission to the truth of what God has said.

> *Fear, worry, and anxiety are seeking to steal our peace, and we cannot permit it.*

God's Word is the ultimate *authority* in our lives. We are bringing the authority "onto the scene" to take these thoughts captive. His Word has authority to *disarm and capture* the false arguments, bringing them into submission. The authority is in the *truth* God has given us in His Word.

We also must recognize the authority given to us through the *name* of Yeshua. In His name, we actively resist and silence the enemy and his lies. We take authority over thoughts that are contrary to God's Word and character. Remember, God is not the source of false arguments that challenge the truth of His Word. Thus, we can take authority over these thoughts, commanding false arguments to be silent in the name of Yeshua. Furthermore, we *speak peace* to our souls, declaring the truths of God's Word. Again, while this is a *spiritual* battle, we engage in the battle with our *minds*.

RESIST BELIEVING FALSE ARGUMENTS

God's Word instructs us regarding anxiety, fear, worry, and more. We are consistently told, "*Do not* be anxious" (Phil. 4:6), "*Do not* be afraid" (Rev. 1:17), "*Do not* worry" (Matt. 6:25), and "*Do not* fear" (Luke 12:7). I have cited only a single verse for each exhortation, but there are dozens more that could be listed. What we must see is that God is *commanding* us in these areas. These are destructive mindsets that are not from Him, thus, we must resist them.

Anxiety, fear, and worry are mindsets that result from believing false arguments. The false arguments of fear and anxiety war against the stance of *faith* God calls us to walk in. Remember, it's only through *faith* that we have access to the *grace* of God. It's His grace that we most need when we are tempted to give in to fear or anxiety. It's only through *faith* that we can know His *peace* when anxiety or fear makes more sense. Experiencing His peace is God's grace to us, and remember, grace typically does not make sense.

Thus, we must learn to deal with the false arguments that present themselves to us day by day. We also need to recognize the *spiritual dimension* of these arguments. What do I mean by that? While the "argument" *begins* as a thought, when we give our attention to the thought, it can take on a life of its own, so to speak.

For example, you might be dealing with a problem or crisis, and a thought comes to your mind suggesting potential negative outcomes of the situation. At such times, we might sense feelings of worry or fear beginning to intensify, eventually growing to the point of our feeling almost *gripped* by anxiety or fear. The reason it can grow from a simple thought to a gripping fear is that there is spiritual power connected to these thoughts. Sometimes, a demonic presence is the *source* of the thought. Other times, it just originates from our own minds. In either case, the more we give our attention to the thought, the more susceptible we are to the power of fear or anxiety gaining a foothold in our lives.

The process begins with a simple thought, but the thought leads to a false argument that challenges our stance of faith and trust. We can see this process all the way back in the events of Genesis 3, where the serpent presents a false narrative to Eve. The serpent sought to convince Eve that she really did not have to obey God's instructions about not eating from the tree of the knowledge of good and evil. He suggests to Eve that God's motive could not be trusted. While she briefly debates with the serpent, ultimately he is successful, as seen in the fact that Eve did choose to defy God's instructions.

We cannot allow ourselves to "dialogue" with, or entertain, lies, either about God or ourselves. We must reject false arguments absolutely and forcefully rather than giving them any consideration. Too often, rather than rejecting the thought and "tearing down" the false argument, we allow it to play out in our minds. When we allow this process rather than resisting and rejecting the worry or fear, we give place to the false argument. By reflecting on fear and anxiety rather than resisting it, we *empower* anxiety. Our *agreement* with deception actually gives *authority* to deception in our lives. It's not our intent, but it does happen if we do not resist the false arguments.

> *We cannot allow ourselves to "dialogue" with, or entertain, lies, either about God or ourselves.*

The false arguments I have described thus far are thoughts based on circumstances we are actually dealing with. In other words, we are *experiencing* some problem or challenge, and the *reality* of the problem is the basis for the anxious thoughts. Understand that there can also be times when the false arguments are not based on what is actually happening. Let me share an example of this.

As human beings, we tend to take what is simple and make it complicated. As this relates to worry and anxiety we might find ourselves exaggerating the size of a problem, allowing it to become larger in our minds than it truly is. In doing this, we end up encouraging and even justifying our fears rather than resisting them in trust and faith. My wife, Jo (who is a woman of strong faith), would sometimes experience this in the earlier days of our marriage. Here, she describes this type of experience in her own words:

> Growing up, I constantly battled fear in my thoughts. Even after coming to the Lord the battle continued, especially when it came to my husband and our children. Fear thoughts would suddenly grip me, seem-

ingly out of nowhere. They would accelerate to the point of paralyzing me in a matter of minutes. As an example, if Jerry was running a little late in coming home from work, I would have a brief thought of wondering why he was late. That thought would quickly be followed by questions about his safety. Within seconds, that brief thought would begin its slide down the slippery slope of fear. I would then begin to imagine Jerry being involved in a major car accident, first picturing an ambulance, then planning his funeral, and finally wondering about my future. All within a matter of minutes! When Jerry would finally come home, I would be a basket case, crying and so thankful he was OK. He had no idea what had happened.

We can laugh about this now, but back then I found that pattern often repeating itself, especially when it involved our children. My mind would automatically go to the worst-case scenario before I even knew what was happening. Then the Lord began to teach me about renewing my thinking with His Word. I learned about taking every thought captive and not giving fear thoughts such freedom to attack my faith and rule my emotions. I learned I could trust God with my children's lives, as well as my husband's and mine. Once I grabbed hold of this truth I found I was able to experience peace as I rejected fear. I was able to draw from my faith in the One who is greater. Over time, I began to walk in victory whenever fear threatened to overwhelm me.

I suspect Jo's experience may not be so uncommon. Many might find themselves fighting a similar battle, but as believers we do not have to settle for anything less than God's peace. Jo learned valuable lessons on the importance of "taking every thought captive" in the battle against anxiety and fear. Our anxieties can seem valid when we process them with logic and reason. But trust and faith, based on the faithfulness of God and the integrity of His Word, will enable us to overcome.

In a previous chapter, I mentioned that we must allow *God* to rule in the realm of our minds and emotions. We could say that the peace of God will fill us as *His* mind prevails over our natural thinking. Jo had unintentionally allowed the false argument to play out in her mind. It began as a thought but grew into something larger until she learned the practice of taking every thought captive. In Jo's case, the false argument was related to fear. But not everyone struggles with fear specifically. For some, a simple discouraging thought can take on a life of its own and escalate to the point of hopelessness.

Here are some simple questions for us to consider:

1. First, we must *identify* thoughts we entertain that contradict God's Word. Ask the question: What are the *types* of thoughts that seem to have the power to rob us of God's peace?
2. Next, identify "triggers" that seem to *stimulate* false arguments we repeatedly find ourselves believing.
3. Finally, consider if there are there certain situations or types of comments that typically affect us negatively, leading us to tolerate false arguments?

We should ask the Holy Spirit to give us discernment on these issues. If we can recognize, in our own lives, patterns in these areas, this can be a valuable step toward being *alert* to the patterns and taking the thoughts captive. But we cannot be passive! Remember, there is a spiritual dimension to fear, anxiety, and every other false argument that comes against us.

We will not battle the thoughts effectively if we try to do so on a purely natural level. So how can we battle these thoughts?

IT IS WRITTEN

Consider Yeshua when He was tested in the wilderness while fasting for forty days. The devil came to Him with a false argument, suggesting He needed to show His power by turning stones into bread so He could have food to eat. Yeshua *immediately* rejected the argument, declaring the Word of God: "It is written, 'Man shall not live by bread alone, but by every word that comes from the mouth of God'" (Matt. 4:4).

In our own lives, the false arguments we deal with might just come from our own minds, but again, they often are demonically inspired. Either way, we need to quickly and firmly resist these arguments as we see that they do not line up with God's Word and God's character. We cannot be passive about such things!

Remember that in these false arguments there is spiritual power to draw us into anxiety, fear, or other debilitating types of mindsets. Have you ever, when attacked in these areas, tried to *talk* yourself out of fear or anxiety, trying to convince yourself that there is really no reason to be fearful or anxious? It doesn't work very well. That's *because* there is a spiritual dimension to such thoughts, and they cannot be overcome by the strength of our minds and logic alone.

> *We will not experience breakthrough and victory over gripping fear or anxiety just by trying to convince ourselves that the fear is unwarranted.*

We will not experience breakthrough and victory over gripping fear or anxiety just by trying to convince ourselves that the fear is unwarranted. Such an approach is attempting to fight a spiritual battle with natural or fleshly weapons. At times when we are being attacked by fear we must learn to see things from heaven's perspective. As I have referenced King David throughout these chapters, we have seen that he had a keen understanding of this heavenly perspective. One verse I love is Psalm 61:2, where he writes, "From the end of the earth I will cry to You, when my heart is overwhelmed; lead me to the rock that is higher than I" (NKJV).

I appreciate David's transparency here. He did not deny *feeling* overwhelmed, but he knew he needed to see things from heaven's higher vantage point. The heavenly perspective we desire, and the power to break through fear and anxiety, comes from the Word of God. Remember, as we considered in the previous chapter, Yeshua described His words as "spirit and life" (John 6:63). In other words, God's Word is filled with *spiritual power* to combat false arguments and strongholds.

This is why it is so important for us to learn God's Word. I'm not just talking about learning the basic narrative, events, and theology of the Bible. Yes, that is essential, but beyond that, we must familiarize ourselves with the multitude of promises in Scripture that describe what God *wants and is committing Himself to do* on behalf of His sons and daughters. In the specific area focused on in this chapter, we should learn the promises God gives us for experiencing peace amid crisis. We should learn the promises related to victory over fear. And then, it is relevant in *all* situations to know and declare the promises of God related to His own nature and character. Exodus 34:6–7 is one of the great passages worth memorizing, as God describes Himself to Moses.

Our knowledge of the true character and nature of God will fill us with greater confidence in His *desire* to fulfill His promises in every area of our lives. God's Word truly has the power to tear down the false arguments and the "fortress walls" that protect the strongholds of fear and anxiety. His Word supernaturally *displaces* wrong thinking and *builds* us in His truth. Thus, David could write with confidence, "In the multitude of my anxieties within me, Your comforts delight my soul" (Ps. 94:19, NKJV). He knew and experienced the power of God to bring comfort to his soul amid the false arguments of fear and anxiety. David was able to experience supernatural peace, even when his circumstances gave him reason to feel anxious.

HELPFUL, PRACTICAL STEPS

Remember, the devil targets our minds and our thought process. A passive mind will be an easy target for the enemy's lies and influence. Thus, it is helpful to form habits that will help us bring our minds under the influence of godly thinking.

In my own life, I have found that the best time to do this is when I awake in the morning. This is important because the early moments of our day often set the tone for the rest of the day. This is also a time when we might be a little less guarded with our thoughts because it can take a few minutes to fully wake up. At times, I find that even before I get out of bed a barrage of negative thoughts try to pull me down. Those thoughts can take the form of complaints or frustrations from the previous day or concerns or worries about the current day and beyond. At that point, my thinking is not yet sharp and clear. I know such thoughts are from the enemy, who seeks to weigh me down before my day even begins.

These are times when the exhortation to take "every thought captive" becomes so important because the enemy seeks to plant negative thoughts in our minds from the moment we wake up. We must learn to seize these early moments of the day by consciously bringing our hearts and minds under the Lord's influence and leadership. Doing this might not come naturally at first, but it really does not take long to form healthy habits in this regard.

The first thing I seek to do when I awake is to quietly offer praise to God, just giving Him thanks for who He is and for His presence in my life. I thank Him that His mercies are new every morning. I usually do not *feel* particularly spiritual at this point of the day, but honestly, that does not matter.

I am *directing my thoughts* toward the Lord and His goodness. I am taking charge of the focus of my thinking. This is something I have gotten into the *habit* of doing. It's part of a daily *routine* I have done now for years. We can typically think of a routine or habit as a negative thing when applied to aspects of our *relationship* with God. But I am taking charge of my thoughts, and as such, it's OK if it feels a bit mechanical when I begin. Remember, the alternative is passivity, and that leaves us open to negative influences through our thoughts or emotions. By directing my thoughts to the Lord, even if initially there is little feeling involved, I am building a fortress wall, so to speak, for keeping out the enemy's lies.

SOME DAILY DECLARATIONS

Once I have been awake for a few minutes and my mind is clearing, I begin what I call my "daily declarations." I do this *while* I am showering, getting dressed, etc. In other words, it's not a *focused* time of prayer or worship, but rather a conversational time of directing my thoughts to the Lord as I am doing other things. Here are the four steps of my "daily declarations":

1. **I begin by declaring my need for God, thanking the Holy Spirit for His presence and help.** I remind myself of my absolute need for God's grace, and I thank Him for His promise of grace for every need. In declaring my need, I am humbling my heart before Him, opening the way for receiving the grace He promises to those who would humble themselves (see James 4:6).

2. **Second, I declare my dependence on the Lord.** While *need* speaks of my condition, *dependence* is about the action I take in response to my need. I tell the Lord that I want to look to Him and not myself for everything pertaining to life and godliness. I usually take a moment to consciously reject the deception of self-sufficiency. If I am looking to the Lord and not to myself, my dependence frees me from *striving* to live a life pleasing to Him.

3. **Third, I declare my gratitude to God.** As I have discussed, gratitude is a key aspect of opening our hearts to the light of His wisdom. I choose thanksgiving as the posture of my heart each day. I remind myself that God Himself is always worthy of my gratitude, so I choose to be thankful, regardless of how I feel. My circumstances do not change God's worthiness to receive honor and thanks from me. I consciously reject every form of complaining, self-pity, and all that wars against a thankful heart.

4. **Finally, I declare my trust in God.** I choose trust, even when I might not understand things that are

happening in my life. I choose trust in spite of the fact that I might have many unanswered questions at any given time. I trust the Lord in spite of any feelings of disappointment or unmet expectations. I trust Him for the simple reason that He is totally trustworthy. I reject the idea of needing to have everything figured out as a basis for my peace of mind. I choose to trust God with my life and with the multitude of things I still have not figured out. Putting my trust in God, I receive His peace that is superior to understanding.

Again, I make these declarations as I'm preparing to start my day. It takes just a couple minutes, although if I want to take more time, I can certainly do that. This is not something that needs to be scheduled as one more task to be added into our already-busy lives. It is simply a time for getting our focus on the Lord and receiving His peace as we do so.

Another helpful practice is to get into the habit, when necessary, of *speaking* to your soul. We see this in the psalms, and it can be quite effective at times when we are experiencing the pull of worry or fear. The psalmist writes, "Why are you cast down, *O my soul?* And why are you disquieted within me? Hope in God, for I shall yet praise Him for the help of His countenance" (Ps. 42:5, NKJV, italics added). Elsewhere we read, "Return to your rest, *my soul*, for Adonai has been good to you" (Ps. 116:7, italics added). Sometimes we just have to speak to ourselves and tell our souls to come into line with God's Word. Doing so can help us refocus and rise above passivity when we feel anxious or fearful.

Another important issue is related to the *pace* of our lives. Clearly, the pace of our culture is such that stress and anxiety has almost become the norm for people today. Depending on our particular circumstances, it can be a challenge to slow down in light of schedules and responsibilities. But what we *can* do is get in the habit of *resting* in His presence amid busy-ness. This is not meant to replace the scheduled daily times we need for focused prayer and reading Scripture, but we can discipline ourselves during our day to take time to consciously step back and look to the Lord. We are exhorted in Psalm 46:11 to *"Be still,* and know that I am God…" (italics added). Stillness helps us refocus on God and become more aware of His presence. God's peace is indeed supernatural, and as such, it is powerful to overcome fear and anxiety. But if we are not *looking* to the Lord, our experience of His peace will be lacking.

One aspect of stepping back and looking to God involves talking directly to Holy Spirit, realizing that the Bible shows Him to be personal. Actually, we should talk to Him *throughout* our day, but I'm referring here to times when we make a point of stepping back from a hectic pace. Ask Him to fill you with His peace. Especially if we are being tempted with fear, we can ask God's Spirit to minister to our hearts the perfect love of the Father that *drives out* fear (see 1 John 4:18). Ask Him to release His divine power to strengthen your mind and emotions with the power of His love (see Ephesians 3:16–19).

> *Sometimes we just have to speak to ourselves and tell our souls to come into line with God's Word.*

The peace of God is a powerful work of God's Spirit. His peace *guards and protects* our hearts and minds as we receive His grace in this area. The work of this supernatural peace is meant to be a steadying force in our lives—not *only* for times when we are tempted with anxiety or fear. His peace steadies us when tempted with insecurity, jealousy, offense, or anger. His peace steadies us when we are being criticized or rejected. It steadies us amid any of the storms of this life the enemy uses to challenge our faith and confidence in God.

Remember, we cannot be passive in relation to "false arguments." Because these lies of worry, anxiety, and fear have demonic spiritual power, they must be *opposed* with a spiritual power that is greater—the Word of God, which Paul refers to as "the sword of the Spirit" (Eph. 6:17). In other words, the Spirit of God uses the "sword" of His Word to render powerless every false argument that wars against our faith. Just as our agreement with the enemy empowers his lies, our agreement with God and His promises to us empowers the working of those promises. Never forget Yeshua's words: "*Do not let* your heart be troubled..." (John 14:1, italics added). The decision is ours to *choose* God's *peace* rather than yield to fear.

Chapter Ten

SUPERNATURAL JOY BEYOND WORDS

I n Romans 14:17, Paul identifies three key foundational aspects of God's work of grace in the believer. He identifies righteousness, peace, and joy as works of the Spirit in our lives. Thus far, we have considered the *righteousness* we cannot earn and the *peace* that is beyond understanding and reason. We now come to the third foundational work which is *joy*. Peter describes this as "joy that is glorious and beyond words" (1 Peter 1:8).

I see joy as a work of the Spirit that brings an *energizing* to our lives. God's joy is far more than just a happy feeling. Joy ministers to us a powerful encouragement to keep moving forward in God's vision for our lives, even when it feels like everything is working against us. Joy gives us the *strength and endurance* we so need for life's journey. As we have already been considering, this journey of life involves ups and downs.

It involves triumphs and challenges. In the writing of James, we find invaluable advice related to joy:

> Consider it all joy, my brethren, when you encounter various trials, knowing that the testing of your faith produces endurance. And let endurance have its perfect work, so that you may be perfect and complete, lacking in nothing. But if any of you lacks wisdom, let him ask of God, who gives to all without hesitation and without reproach; and it will be given to him (James 1:2–5).

James presents an idea here that can seem unrealistic and perhaps even unreachable to us. He tells us we are to "consider it all joy" as we go through trials and unpleasant circumstances. Notice what he does *not* say here. He does not tell us, "Don't get discouraged" or "Don't get down about your trials." Why?

We are not to open the door of our hearts to the poison of complaining, self-pity, and other attitudes that can pull us down.

Because he is not addressing us in the area of our *emotions*. What he *is* doing is addressing us in the area of our will. Or we could say he is addressing us in the area of our *faith*, because we are to *believe and trust* that in times of trial and adversity there is actually *reason* for joy. James even urges us to consider it *all* joy. Why is that important? I believe he is emphasizing the idea of not settling for a *mixture* of joy and negativity. We are not to open the door of our hearts to the poison of complaining, self-pity, and other attitudes that can pull us down. Rather, we must settle it in our minds that the trials we go through are *opportunities* for joy.

Clearly, none of us will escape the reality of trials and adversity in this life. But think about what James is telling us. He is presenting a concept of *victory* amid our trials. It's a victory that can be very different from our own concept. *Our* idea of victory usually involves *getting out* of the problems we are experiencing, but James is showing us that victory is based largely on what is going on *within* us. Victory is not necessarily based on our circumstances changing, even though that is often what we most desire. Certainly there *are* times when victory involves a change in our circumstances. Perhaps we are experiencing some sort of hardship, and God intervenes to deliver us from the hardship or bring a breakthrough. We love these types of victories, and we should indeed be praying for them. But James is talking here about victory on a different level.

First, he tells us to *consider* it joy when we encounter trials. I think if we are being totally honest we would acknowledge that joy is not our *natural reaction* when we experience the trials of life. Joy is not usually our first response. Here is what we must draw from this—if joy is not our *natural* reaction to adversity, then clearly, we need *grace from God* to be *able* to consider it all joy at such times. We need *grace* for doing this *because* it does not come naturally to us.

We can find a similar exhortation from Paul, as he tells us, "we rejoice in our sufferings, knowing that suffering produces endurance, and endurance produces character, and character produces hope" (Rom. 5:3–4, ESV). Paul and James are making a similar point—they both connect *joy* and *endurance* to the trials we go through. Notice that James does not tell us to *feel* joyful. He tells us to *consider* it joy when we encounter trials. Again, joy involves our *will*. It involves a *faith determination* to *be* a people of joy, even amid adversity and trials.

The parallel verses from Romans reveal a key for *experiencing* joy in trials, as Paul says we are to "rejoice" in tribulation. As we considered in a previous chapter, rejoicing is the *faith action that releases* joy in us. Rejoicing is not something we do only *because* we feel joyful. It is a faith act that expresses our *love and trust for God*, even when things are not going the way we would like. Too often we can reverse the process, thinking, "I will rejoice when I *feel* joyful."

We must see that rejoicing is a faith act that is a choice of our will. It's a decision we make in spite of the fact that we might not *like* the circumstances we are dealing with. This really is a major issue for us. We must understand that our overall state of mind is directed either by our outward circumstances or our *trust* for God. Our mindset will be determined by either discouragement and anxiety or faith and trust, and rejoicing moves us in the direction of faith and trust.

GRACE FOR EXPERIENCING JOY

There is a *grace* from God for us to be able to *have joy*, even in trials or suffering. One of the most powerful expressions of *victory* for believers is seen as we learn to *maintain our joy*, regardless of what we might be going through in our lives.

We can struggle in this area because, too often, we do not even *consider* joy as something we are *looking* for amid trials. If we are honest about it, more often than not, we are just looking to get out from under the problems. We are usually looking for *relief* or an end to the trial. Now, it's normal to think that way, to desire relief. There is nothing wrong with that response, and it's certainly not something to feel condemnation about. But here is what I believe we must see—we can end up *missing the grace* that God provides for *joy* amid trials if we do not *look* for joy, but instead, look for relief alone.

I began this book by citing Romans 5:2, where Paul instructs us that it is *by faith* that we *enter into* the grace God has for our lives. Clearly, faith is something that is *intentional*. Faith is not something we get by accident, but we grow in faith as we are *intentional* about agreeing with and acting on God's Word.

So, we must be intentional about *being* joyful. Because the Bible tells us to consider it joy when we go through trials, then we can assume that God will give us *grace* for that joy. Of course, we really do *need* grace for experiencing joy when our circumstances are unpleasant. But again, a problem is that too often joy is not one of the "options" we *see* as God's grace when we are experiencing adversity. We usually think God's grace means *getting me out* of the discomfort or pain of what I am going through. When we just look for *relief*, we can miss the *grace* God has for *joy* in the trial because we are not necessarily *looking* for joy in that moment or season.

Amid trials and adversities, when we can be tempted with discouragement and even giving up, *joy* is our *greatest need*. Joy is a key to getting through the trials with the *fullness* of victory God wants us to experience. You see, it's *perspective* that we must take hold of when we are going through difficult seasons. Why? Because perspective helps us see that there is *value* in what we are going through, even though we may not enjoy it. Joy is what empowers us for this process. Too often, we are so focused on the trial itself, or the "wilderness" we feel we are going through, that we do not see what God is doing, or wanting to do, in those times.

ARE WE LEARNING?

What should we look for and learn as we go through trials? We can gain valuable insight as we consider the words of Moses. Following Israel's forty years of wilderness wandering, Moses gave these instructions prior to the people entering the Promised Land:

> And you shall remember the whole way that the LORD your God has led you these forty years in the wilderness, that he might *humble* you, *testing* you to know what was in your heart, whether you would keep his commandments or not. And he humbled you and let you hunger and fed you with manna... that he *might make you know* that man does not live by bread alone, but man lives by every word that comes from the mouth of the LORD. Your clothing did not wear out on you and your foot did not swell these forty years. Know then in your heart that, as a man disciplines his son, the LORD your God *disciplines* you (Deuteronomy 8:2–5 ESV, italics added).

I believe we can see here that God has several goals in view for *us* as we deal with trials, crises, and difficult circumstances. Here are four:

1. First, Moses cites humility. God seeks to *humble* us, and He does so through adversities that challenge

and expose our self-sufficiency as well as our need. Humility indeed requires lifelong lessons we are to be learning, lessons central to the formation of Messiah-like character.

2. Then, He sees our trials as times of *testing*. Unlike our formal education in school, God's testing is not just to determine whether or not we know the right answers. God tests us to show us what is *in our hearts*.

3. Third, our times of trial are times when God is *teaching* us.

4. Finally, God *disciplines* us through challenges and adversity.

When we are humbled, tested, taught, and disciplined we can be tempted to interpret these processes from a negative mindset. But Moses points out two important truths that provided necessary perspective for Israel:

1. First, he reminds them that through the entire wilderness experience God never failed to supernaturally provide for the Israelites. They did not always get what they *wanted,* but they never lacked what they *needed.*

2. Second, Moses points out God's place of fathering with Israel as the backdrop for the discipline He brought to them. Thus, in our trials and even times of suffering, there is *supernatural provision*, and there is God's *fathering presence.*

These are key truths meant to give us proper perspective and encouragement as we go through life's challenges.

Through a life and mindset of worship and honoring God we can cultivate a joy in our hearts, regardless of what we are going through. That joy is what positions us to recognize what *God* is doing, rather than just focusing on how hard we feel our circumstances are. If we do not come into the place of considering it all joy through rejoicing in trials, then we will ultimately learn little or nothing *through* our times of trials.

LEARNING IN THE SCHOOL OF YESHUA

I have come to believe that everything God does and everything He allows in our lives is meant for a purpose. That purpose is to expose to us our *need* for Him, as well as seeing whether or not *we recognize* that need. If we go through life never truly learning our utter need for God and His grace, we will surely miss out on life's most important lessons, as well as life's greatest victories. Plus, we will find ourselves inadequate for anything God calls us to be and do.

> *Yeshua knew Peter's heart, and He knew that Peter himself needed to discover his own heart.*

What we go through in life is all about *discovery* of our need. This is how Yeshua Himself taught His disciples. He allowed them to go through crises so they would discover necessary truths. For example, Yeshua knew they would experience severe opposition. He knew they would have to be steadfast in their allegiance and devotion to Him. Therefore, the disciples themselves had to learn that they could not lean on their *natural* human devotion and sincerity if they wanted to persevere as His disciples. They had to come to the place of seeing their need for God's grace, which alone could take them *beyond* their natural abilities.

Consider the conversation between Peter and Yeshua, when Yeshua warned Peter that he would deny Him three times (see Matthew 26:34). Peter responded by insisting he could never deny the Lord (v. 35). Peter's devotion was certainly real, and he was sincere in his insistence. But Yeshua *knew* Peter's heart, and He knew that Peter himself needed to *discover* his own heart. This was not so that Peter would feel condemned or like he was a total failure. It was to expose to Peter his own need so that he would look beyond his *natural* ability and devotion for fulfilling the calling God had for his life. The only way Peter would learn this lesson was for him to experience the crisis of his own failure.

There is another conversation between Yeshua and Simon Peter that is worth revisiting. We considered this back in chapter 6, as we were examining the principle that God sees us for what we are becoming. Some additional observations are especially relevant to the issue of gaining perspective amid trials. Yeshua said, "Simon, Simon! Indeed satan has demanded to sift you all like wheat. But *I have prayed for you*, Simon, that your *faith will not fail*. And when you have turned back, strengthen your brothers" (Luke 22:31–32, italics added).

I should note what Yeshua did *not* do here. He did not say, "Don't worry, Simon. I would never allow something like this to happen to you." In other words, Yeshua did not suggest He would *shield* Simon Peter from *going through* the "sifting" He was warning him about. Consider what Yeshua *does* say to Peter. He says, "I have prayed for you, Simon, that your faith will not fail." He then tells Peter of His confidence that, after Peter has gone through the crisis—after denying Yeshua three times—he would repent and *return* to his faith and even to his role of leadership among the disciples. Peter would become a source of *strengthening* to the others.

What can we glean from this exchange? Four key points stand out to me from Yeshua's words:

1. **Yeshua *allowed* the sifting.** I believe He did so to expose to Peter his own weakness and need. As we look in hindsight at the magnitude of Peter's calling, we can see why it was so important for him to recognize his areas of weakness. Peter's eyes had to be opened to issues that would prevent him from maturing as a godly man of character, as well as a foundational leader in the body of Messiah.

2. **Peter's flaws did not prevent Yeshua from recognizing, affirming, and even prophesying, Peter's destiny.** Peter's failure did not disqualify him. That is good news for every one of *us*.

3. **Yeshua was confident that Peter would *make it***

through **the trial victoriously.** We can easily *miss* this in the verses because Yeshua's words to Peter are quite weighty. What is clear is that Yeshua *fully believed* in Peter to be victorious. Yeshua's confidence was not based on *Peter's* own strengths but in God's mercy and grace to be Peter's strength amid the trial. God is committed to accomplishing, in us and through us, what we cannot do in our own strength. I believe Yeshua saw Peter's heart, and He knew Peter would ultimately respond with humility, repentance, and faith. The trial Peter would go through would actually become a context for *Peter* to see that *Yeshua had faith* that Peter would be victorious.

4. *Yeshua's intercession* **for Peter is a glorious truth.** Interestingly, Yeshua's prayer was that Peter's *faith* would not fail. I suspect that Peter, while processing his personal failure, was *tempted* to give up, and surely Yeshua was aware of that possibility.

Sometimes, as we go through various trials of life, we might find ourselves wondering if *we* will make it through. How encouraging it is to know that Yeshua is interceding for *us*, and He believes we will make it through victoriously! Although our personal *preference* might be that the Lord would *shield* us from the trials that can be so distasteful, He has a *better* plan that leads us into victory and destiny. He is even praying us through the process.

WHAT IS OUR RESPONSE?

Here is something for us to see in Peter's experience, and this is relevant to every one of us as believers. The "tests" that we go through in our journey of faith are not so that *God* can see if we will pass. He already knows the answer to that, and He already knows the condition of our hearts. Rather, the trials and tests are meant to provide a context for *us* to recognize the true condition of *our own hearts*. Then, from that point, our *response* to seeing our own hearts can end up setting a course for our lives. Peter's greatest *failure* became the context for some of the most significant life *lessons* to be learned. Ultimately, his crisis became the context for the biggest steps forward in his life, launching him into his calling and destiny.

When we respond to trials by declaring, in essence, "Lord, I don't necessarily like what I am going through, but in the midst of it, I want to declare Your goodness and faithfulness. I want to declare my trust in You and my allegiance to You. I choose to *rejoice* in who You are, and I commit to *learning* what You want me to learn in this."

> **Peter's greatest failure became the context for some of the most significant life lessons to be learned.**

That kind of response can set a course for our lives that is powerful, declaring that nothing of this world can ultimately defeat our faith. However, if we respond to trials with complaining and self-pity, that response sets a course in a different direction. I'm not talking here about *moments* of complaining or self-pity. Every one of us has likely experienced the temptation to slip into these negative attitudes. I'm talking about *remaining* in a mindset of complaining or self-pity and not moving on from that.

EMBRACING PROCESS

Our lives on this Earth are all about *process* and *preparation*. Understanding this should give us fuller *perspective* amid the trials we experience. As stated previously, God sees our lives based on the truth of what we are *becoming* by His grace. We must always keep in mind that we are in the process of *becoming* something. We are on a *journey* that is *taking* us somewhere. Our *responses* to the events of life are key in determining what our destination will look like.

Although God does indeed have a destiny and purpose for each of us, we have a role to play in *coming into* that destiny. Our decisions and choices really do matter. Our faith and obedience are crucial. If we consistently respond to the events of our journey with complaining, unbelief, and skepticism, we are not likely to fulfill a destiny that calls for faith and obedience. God is amazingly gracious and patient in working with us, but He will not override our will if we are continually resisting what He is seeking to do in our lives.

Of course, on the most foundational level, as we have already considered, the destination to which God is taking us is about our *becoming* more like Yeshua. We are being conformed into His likeness "from glory to glory" (see 2 Corinthians 3:18). *This is* the *ultimate* destination for every believer—the *ultimate goal* God has for our lives. A *lifelong process* is involved for *arriving* at this destination, and unfortunately, the process does involve hardships and trials. No one ever just *arrives* at this destination without going through the process, because it's the *process* that God uses to shape and mold us on the inside. In our natural thinking and impatience, we would like to just *arrive* at our destination without the process, but that will not happen.

ALL THINGS WORK TOGETHER?

A key Scripture for gaining insight into this issue is Romans 8:28–29: "Now we know that all things work together for good for those who love God, who are called according to His purpose. For those whom He foreknew He also predestined to be conformed to the image of His Son..."

This verse is often misunderstood and wrongly applied. Sometimes it is pulled out of context and used to suggest that because God is good, everything will just end up working out OK. Such words are usually well intended for encouraging someone going through a hard time, but that misrepresents what the passage actually means. The key phrase for properly interpreting the passage is "called according to His purpose." Then, in the following verse, Paul *tells* us what that purpose is—we are "to be conformed to the image of (God's) Son." That is the Lord's most basic goal for the life of every believer.

So, here is what I believe we are to see in these verses. For those who love God and *embrace* this ultimate calling to be conformed into Yeshua's image, we can be confident that God can use everything that happens in our lives to accomplish that purpose. In *that specific sense*, all things do work together for the good of building in us a likeness to our Messiah. God will use even the bad things that might happen to us, and through it all, He does a work *within* us that deepens our love or strengthens our character. I'm not suggesting that God *initiates* the bad things, but He certainly can and does work *through* them. By the work of His grace and the power of His Spirit, He builds us up on the inside, helping us *respond* with *godliness* amid adversity. The *process* becomes a part of the formation of the likeness to Yeshua that we seek.

So, when we love God, and the goal of becoming like Messiah is *our* highest goal, we can be encouraged that God uses everything we go through for *accomplishing* that goal in us. Now, that is *really good news* because it means that nothing of this world can ultimately defeat us, assuming that *our* goal is the same as God's goal. But if our goal is just to avoid hardship and live an easy or comfortable life, then we can end up seeing trials only for the inconvenience they cause. As such, the process, which is *meant* for our growth, can end up becoming more of a stumbling block to us because we don't see it in light of *God's* purpose to bring forth a likeness to His Son.

Here is the bottom line: God causes everything we go through to work together for good, in relation to *our becoming* conformed into Yeshua's likeness. Thus, as *we respond* to everything we go through with a heartfelt desire to *become* more like Him, then God will use the things we go through to work together *for* that goal.

BECOMING LIKE YESHUA—THE INCONVENIENT TRUTH

Here is a challenge we all face. In every area where *God* is conforming us to Yeshua's likeness, there will always be something of *self* that has to die. Why? Because the one thing that ultimately interferes with my becoming like Yeshua, is *me*—my pride, my stubbornness, my desires, my love for comfort, my selfishness, and more—it all has to die! And God knows how to set us up for recognizing the areas of our self-life that are getting in the way.

Remember, God's highest concern is for what we are *becoming*, not for our comfort or convenience. In fact, I think it's almost certain that everything important that God does in our lives for shaping us into that likeness to Yeshua comes in the midst of the *dis*comfort and *in*convenience we try so hard to avoid. I think probably *every aspect* of likeness to Yeshua is realized in the midst of inconvenience.

A few examples come to mind. We learn to be people of *love*, as we are confronted with the challenge of *un*lovable people. We learn to be people of *purity and holiness* as we are confronted with the *discomfort* of saying no to unhealthy fleshly desires. We learn to be people of *boldness*, as we are confronted with the resistance, and even hostility, of people who do not want to hear the message we share. We learn to be people of *humility*, as we are confronted with the challenges of setting aside our egos and pride. We learn to be a people who *forgive* as we are confronted with the pain of being mistreated. And yes, we learn to be a people of *joy* as we are confronted with those trials of life that can be so unpleasant.

> *He is fully committed to empowering us with His presence, for going through the inconveniences He so often uses in our transformation.*

Clearly, it is not God's goal to make things convenient for us. He *is* fully *committed* to empowering us with His presence, for *going through* the *in*conveniences He so often uses in our transformation. That is the *grace* we can miss when we are so focused on the *discomfort* of the trials and our desire for relief.

When we face trials one of the *wrong responses* we can have is to conclude something like, "God just isn't doing anything to help me out here..." While we might indeed *feel* like that at times, such an attitude is quite detrimental to us. As long as we *think* God is not doing anything in our lives, especially as we go through adversity, then we open ourselves up to the lie that God has abandoned us. Thus, if all we are looking for is relief from the trial, and we don't *experience* that relief right away, we can wonder, "Has God abandoned me?" But the truth is, He is working in *all* our situations, even when we might *feel* like He is absent.

It is *joy* that sustains and helps us through our trials. It helps us gain perspective of what *God Himself* is doing during those times. Beyond perspective, joy energizes our lives, allowing us to get through trials and adversities victoriously.

Remember, God will give us *grace* for experiencing joy that does not make sense to our natural thinking. That's why we *need* grace for it, and that's why we need the Spirit of God to *fill* us with this joy. But *because* it is a joy that is unnatural and unreasonable, we must be intentional in our mindset and lifestyle of rejoicing. Otherwise, we can miss the grace God gives us for joy, as we look instead for relief alone.

Rejoicing in God is a key response that can help set a course for our lives, so that God is honored in our actions and *reac*-tions to the things we are going through.

CHAPTER ELEVEN

THE POWER OF REJOICING

As we continue our focus on supernatural joy, remember that *rejoicing* is the faith action that *results* in joy, as we persevere in our thanksgiving amid the difficulties we encounter. Let's consider four key practical results that rejoicing brings as we go through trials. Understand that each of these impacts our *thinking* or how we are *seeing* things:

1. **Rejoicing is powerful in *defeating despair*.** In previous chapters, we considered how we can be susceptible at times to "false arguments"—negative thoughts that can take on a life of their own as they impact our minds and emotions. When we go through difficult times, the enemy will try to influence us with thoughts that are clearly destructive. But because we can be unguarded with our thoughts, and more vulnerable during times of trial, we might not be as quick to recognize the source of such false arguments. Thus, they might even sound reasonable to us if our guard is down.

The enemy brings thoughts of discouragement or hopelessness. He tempts us to wonder if God has abandoned us, or if He is just not concerned with our situation. There are so many possible narratives that can lead us into discouragement, and if we dwell on our discouragement, it can take us into a place of real despair. Despair becomes a spiritually empowered influence that must be battled with spiritual power that is greater. Rejoicing has the effect of *breaking* the power of despair, releasing us into hope and joy as we persevere. Perseverance is definitely a key here. The breakthrough, though sometimes immediate, usually requires time and persistence. What we must see is that rejoicing releases God's presence, and therein is our source of victory and breakthrough.

2. **Rejoicing is powerful in *overcoming negativity*.**
   We have already touched on the natural tendency we can have, when going through difficult seasons, to give way to complaining or self-pity. As with any negative mindset, the more we allow ourselves to complain and feel self-pity, it seems that we just get deeper into a mental or emotional rut. It's a challenge to try to talk ourselves out of the rut because our negativity *makes sense* to us. We feel like it's reasonable based on what we are going through. As we sink into negativity, it's as if a fog sets in over our thoughts and emotions, and we can struggle to see things clearly.

   To break away from this, we again need the spiritual breakthrough that the presence of God brings. Rejoicing releases God's presence, bringing us grace to overcome the negativity we've slipped into. It overrides the natural tendency to feel sorry for ourselves and allows us to *see* things more clearly. As we honor God through rejoicing, we can find the "fog" lifting. Rather than feeling trapped in our problems, we can experience grace for seeing things with God's perspective.

3. **Rejoicing is powerful in *breaking through doubt and unbelief.*** During trials, we can begin to entertain doubts. They might be doubts related to ourselves or doubts related to God. We can find ourselves asking all kinds of questions that work against our faith and confidence. "Have I done something wrong for this to be happening? Is God mad at me?" Of course, what we most need at such times is faith and expectation. God's Word is key to *building* faith, but it's rejoicing that can have the effect of opening our hearts to *receive* God's Word. As we exalt the Lord for His greatness as well as His faithfulness, grace is released to enlarge our hearts to *believe* Him for what He is willing and able to do.

4. **Rejoicing *breaks* the power of *anxiety.*** We considered this in depth in previous chapters, but it is also relevant to our being joyful as we navigate trials. Anxious thoughts are clearly a temptation as we go through trials and adversity. When we are feeling overwhelmed by situations for which we lack answers, rejoicing can have the effect of calming our anxious hearts. Rejoicing at such times is a supernaturally inspired faith response that lifts us above the challenge, pain, or confusion of our circumstances. It can lead our hearts to the peace we need for responding properly.

Earlier, I cited Psalm 61:2: "When my heart is overwhelmed, lead me to the rock that is higher than I" (NKJV). When we are "higher up," we have a better vantage point for seeing clearly. Rejoicing and worship lift us up to that higher ground, where our perspective gets clearer. As we do so, we find that our hearts do not have to *remain* overwhelmed.

It is not uncommon, amid trials, for us to try to *figure out* the answers and solutions to the problem(s) we are dealing with. But often, we can feel like those answers are nowhere to be found. At such times, our greatest need is to get our focus away from trying to solve the problem and get our eyes on the One who has *infinite* knowledge and wisdom for every situation. Rejoicing and worship are key to getting our focus on the Lord. When we do so, it impacts us inwardly. When we worship Him amid some trial, it's as if a "light goes on" inside us.

I can attest to this from so many times of personal experience. As we rejoice, we can feel a confidence settling in on our hearts, a sense of *knowing* that God is in control. We don't necessarily get specifics for solving the problems, but we feel a release into peace and faith that God has the answers. It's as if an inner burden lifts from us as we worship, and we receive a sense of encouragement from God's involvement. Nothing has changed outwardly, and because of that, it really doesn't make sense that the burden is lifting. But this attests to the spiritual power released through our worship of God and honoring Him before we can *see* any visible change.

THE ABRAHAM MODEL

In Romans 4, Paul shares valuable insight on the faith walk of Abraham. Of course, God had promised that Abraham and his wife, Sarah, would have a son who would carry the covenant promise, ultimately leading to the coming of Messiah. But for years, there was no fulfillment of that promise. Abraham had reached the age of one hundred, and Sarah had been barren all her life, but in fulfillment of the promise, God miraculously gave them a son, Isaac.

There was no reason, naturally speaking, for Abraham to *expect* this son, except for the fact that God said He would do it. What is key here is Abraham's attitude and actions when there was really no hope. Paul writes, "Yet he did not waver in unbelief concerning the promise of God. Rather, he was strengthened in faith, *giving glory to God*. He was fully convinced that what God has promised, He also is able to do" (Rom. 4:20–21, italics added). Giving glory to God in the middle of the trial, when there really was no hope for the son who had been promised, had the effect of *strengthening the faith* of Abraham. We might say that Abraham's willingness to honor God, when there was no visible evidence for expecting an answer, had the effect of breaking the power of doubt and unbelief and strengthening his faith.

It's helpful to note Paul's wording as he describes the nature of Abraham's faith. He writes that Abraham was "fully convinced" of the certainty of God's promise coming to pass. For Abraham to have been "convinced," or persuaded, suggests that a *process* was involved that led to his certainty. If we are *persuaded* of something, that suggests we had to be moved from one position to another. Why is this important? Because we can be encouraged to see that Abraham did not necessarily *start out* certain. Faith *grew* on the inside, leading him to the point of eventually being *convinced* of God's faithfulness, but he did not begin that way. You might wonder how you could ever have great faith; but be

> *Giving glory to God in the middle of the trial, when there really was no hope for the son who had been promised, had the effect of strengthening the faith of Abraham.*

encouraged that Abraham did not start out as a "faith giant." Over time, as he *gave glory* to God and focused on God's promises, Abraham *became* convinced that God would indeed accomplish what He said He would do.

A few verses earlier, Paul wrote of Abraham, "In hope beyond hope, he trusted that he would become the father of many nations according to what was spoken" (Rom. 4:18). This is such an amazing statement! Think about it. Abraham had no logical reason to expect that he and Sarah would be able to have a son. Their situation was *beyond* the point where hope was even reasonable. Yet Abraham *had hope*, a hope that was nurtured by his willingness to give glory to the Lord for His faithfulness. Without *hope*, we will never be a people of *faith*.

In Hebrews 11, faith is described as "the substance of things *hoped* for" (v. 1). Thus, we can see that hope and faith go together; hope actually *precedes* faith. The writer of Hebrews gives us a powerful description of hope, calling it "an anchor of the soul" (Heb. 6:19). Just as a ship's anchor prevents the ship from drifting, hope has a similar effect on our souls. Hope keeps us from drifting into the dangerous waters of doubt and unbelief.

Rejoicing in the Lord and honoring Him with our worship will strengthen us in hope and faith, helping us remain steady when we feel like our lives are being shaken. It releases joy in our hearts, and that joy strengthens and sustains us amid trials. Rejoicing indeed breaks the power of doubt and unbelief. Our faith and trust are energized and strengthened as the *influence* of unbelief is neutralized by our praise to God.

Aligning our hearts with God's heart is key to gaining the wisdom we so need in trying times.

What we must see is that honoring God through rejoicing is key to getting *our* hearts aligned with *God's* heart. I cannot think of anything more important to us when our faith is challenged through trials and crises. Aligning our hearts with God's heart is key to gaining the wisdom we so need in trying times. I believe our willingness to assume a posture of praise, at times when we do not understand why we are going through adversity, is key to experiencing the fullness of the joy of the Lord. The posture of thanksgiving opens our hearts to receive a supernatural impartation from God's Spirit. Joy is a result of that impartation. When someone is going through trials, yet they maintain an unreasonable joy, that becomes a testimony that draws the attention of others.

ETERNAL PERSPECTIVE

As we draw to a close in our consideration of supernatural joy and receiving *grace* for that joy amid trials, our discussion would be incomplete if we neglected to bring out the words of Peter from his first letter. It is here that we see the *ultimate* reason *why* we can be a people of joy regardless of our circumstances:

An incorruptible, undefiled, and unfading inheritance has been reserved in heaven for you...You rejoice *in this* greatly, even though now for a little while, if necessary, you have been distressed by various trials. These trials are so that the true metal of your faith (far more valuable than gold, which perishes though refined by fire) may come to light in praise and glory and honor at the revelation of Messiah Yeshua. Though you have not seen Him, you love Him. And even though you don't see Him now, you trust Him and are filled with a *joy that is glorious beyond words* (1 Peter 1:4–8, italics added).

Consider the dramatic transformation that obviously took place in Peter. It is a transformation that took him from the cowardice and shame of having denied the Lord to a place of amazing trust and joy *in spite* of the fierce opposition he faced. How can such transformation take place? Much could be said in attempting to explain it, but I think Peter gives us valuable insight through the words of this powerful passage. Clearly, God opened his eyes to gain a glimpse into the *eternal inheritance* in store for every follower of Yeshua. This is something so utterly glorious that everything of this present life pales in comparison. He describes this eternal inheritance with the words "incorruptible, undefiled, and unfading."

Think about the contrasting image these words give us, compared to the nature of life in this present age. Our eternal inheritance is, first, "incorruptible." It cannot in any way be diminished. The idea here is that there is an immortality connected with this inheritance. Unlike the things of this world, it is not subject to decay in any way.

Then he writes that our inheritance is "undefiled," referring to its purity. In other words, it is completely untainted by the sin and death that have infected this world. And then, our inheritance is "unfading." It will not lose its brightness or brilliance but retains its glorious nature forever. No problem, trial, or even tragedy can impose itself with any impact on this eternal inheritance that is being kept for us in heaven. This is what awaits us, and *this is a reason* we can *rejoice greatly*.

Notice that Peter is writing to believers who are dealing with sorrows and trials. His encouragement to them is to *rejoice*, in spite of their distressing trials, as they fix their eyes on the glorious promises of an eternal inheritance. He certainly was not minimizing the difficulties and pain that every human being experiences in this life.

He reminds us that the trials are part of a process that *will* come to an end. However, we have an *eternal* inheritance awaiting us, and *that* inheritance is incorruptible, undefiled, and unfading. Trusting in this, and putting our hope in the *Lord Himself*, we can be filled with a joy that is "glorious beyond words."

Peter's words challenge us to examine what we are ultimately *hoping* in. Sometimes, when faced with adversity, believers can react with surprise, as if hoping that their faith would have shielded them from all problems. But the Bible does not promise us a problem-free life. Sadly, life in this fallen age does include trials and pain, but when our trust is in the Lord, there is a *grace* available to us that sustains and even *energizes* us through the trials. Most importantly, He gives us the blessing of His *presence*. God shows us His mercy, grace, and faithfulness in so many ways throughout the challenges of this life. As we walk with Him and learn of His promises for the age to come, we gain confidence that He will never fail us. His promised eternal inheritance could not possibly leave us disappointed.

I am not suggesting that our only *interest* should be in the promises for the age to come. The Bible gives us so many promises of blessing related to life in this *present* age, and yes, we are to pursue those promises and their fulfillment. But because we live in a fallen world, there is warfare over those promises, and sometimes we do not experience them to the degree we hope and believe for. Entire books are written on this issue, seeking to provide understanding and explanations. That is not our focus here, but I point this out for two basic reasons:

1. **First, we should live our lives seeking and expecting fulfillment of all that God promises for this present life, even though we sometimes experience disappointment.** Placing hope in *eternal* promises is not to suggest that the promises for this age are not worthy of our attention.

2. **Second, we must recognize the *contrast* between the promises for this life and those for the age to come.** Peter's point in the above passage is that, unlike the promises for this life, the eternal promises awaiting us are *beyond the reach* of sin and death, corruption and disappointment, trials and adversity. *Seeing* this contrast is to give us unwavering hope as we go through the difficulties of life in this present age.

If our highest hopes are set on experiencing ultimate fulfillment in *this life*, we will struggle to take hold of the joy to be found in *eternal* perspective. This is why Peter writes later in the chapter that we must "set (our) hope *completely* on the grace that will be brought to (us) at the revelation of Yeshua the Messiah" (1 Peter 1:13, italics added).

Remember, this *present* age is all about *formation* and *preparation* in our lives. That formation and preparation are largely *for* the age to come. If *this* life here and now is all there is, then anxiety, fear, and discouragement do make sense. But if this present life is actually preparation for something far greater, we can be at peace as well as full of joy in every situation.

So again, our ultimate hope is not for a problem-free life here and now. Such a hope will surely lead to disappointment, and even disillusionment. Our ultimate hope is found in the promises of an eternity with the Lord in His unshakable Kingdom. Yeshua is returning for a spotless bride, and as those who love and follow Him, *we are* that bride. He is returning for you and me, and we will be with Him forever. He will establish His Kingdom on Earth, and *we will rule with* Him. After His rule of one thousand years, Yeshua will ultimately defeat and banish every form of evil, sin, sickness, and death, and for us there is coming a time when there will be no more tears or sorrow. There is nothing that has the ability or power to interfere in any way with these promises and so many more that are equally amazing. *This* is the basis for our ultimate hope, and this is the basis for a life of rejoicing.

Do we give much thought to these amazing truths? I suspect we all fall short in this, as the "here and now" seems so much more real to us.

If this is an area of struggle for you, I encourage you, for a season, to make a point of reading daily, or at least regularly, the great chapters of Revelation 21 and 22. Ask the Lord to grip your heart with a fresh and vibrant view of the eternal inheritance waiting for us. Ask Him to fill you with a sense of confidence and faith that would cause these truths to become as real as the things of this life, and even more. There is a joy available to us that is "glorious beyond words," a joy that can fill our hearts and energize us amid life's challenges.

Life indeed includes trials and disappointments, but we do not have to be defeated by our disappointments. *Joy is a key* to our victory. God's intent is for His supernatural joy to become like a lens through which we see all the events of our lives. Joy changes how we see life itself and positions us to have God's perspective in everything we go through. We do not live in denial or just pretend things are good when they are not. But through joy, we position ourselves to *see God* in every step of our journey of life.

Remember, this joy that steadies us and energizes us for life's journey is not something we try to "work up" in our emotions. Rather, it is a joy that comes from God Himself. At a time when Jewish people were returning to Jerusalem from Babylonian exile, they experienced hardship and opposition as they sought to rebuild the city and the Temple. Amid their struggles, we find the great words of Nehemiah, exhorting them, "Do not sorrow, for the joy of the LORD is your strength" (Neh. 8:10b, NKJV). In times when *enjoyment* might be lacking, *joy* becomes a supernatural source of our strength. We must not settle for less.

The words of the prophet Habakkuk are appropriate for concluding this chapter:

> Though the fig tree does not blossom, and there is no yield on the vines, though the olive crop fail, and the fields produce no food, the flock is cut off from the fold, and there is no cattle in the stalls. *Yet will I triumph in Adonai, I will rejoice in the God of my salvation* (Habakkuk 3:17–18, italics added).

God gives us *grace* for rejoicing at times when rejoicing makes no sense. Joy from the Lord has the power to *sustain* us and energize us at times when life's trials give us *reason* to feel overwhelmed. It is joy that enables us to look ahead to our future with hope, even amid trials and crises. Thus, by God's grace of joy, our problems and trials lose their ability to define us or defeat us.

May the Lord bless us with His *grace* for joy in our journey.

CHAPTER TWELVE

WHAT'S THE POINT? LIVING BEYOND OURSELVES

Everything we've considered thus far relates to the power and work of grace *in* our lives as followers of Yeshua. In His vast mercy and love, God embraces us and forgives us in spite of our failures. He imparts to us a *righteousness* that frees us from guilt and shame, enabling us to walk in relationship with God and live according to the design of our Creator. From the security of this life-giving relationship, we can experience supernatural *peace* that steadies us at times when fear would make more sense. Through His grace, we can also walk in unreasonable *joy* that energizes us when the trials of life can leave us feeling weary and discouraged.

What are we to see as the *point* of these powerful works of grace in our lives? Is it simply so we can feel good and blessed for our *own enjoyment?* No, grace does not end with us and our

143

personal blessing alone. *My* blessing is meant to be a beginning point for a life lived *beyond* myself, not just focused *within* myself. Yeshua's own words state the issue simply and clearly: "Freely you received, freely give" (Matt. 10:8b). What *we* have received from the Lord is His blessing *to us,* but then, as a blessed people, we live to *bless others.* As grace abounds in our *own* lives, we are to *impart* grace to those around us (see Ephesians 4:29). You see, *our* calling is to show the world what God is truly like, and we do this by "impart(ing) grace" to people in various ways.

CREATED TO LOVE OTHERS

As discussed in chapter 8, God has created us all for love. Ephesians 3:17 says our lives are to be "rooted and grounded in love." As we *receive* God's love and abide in it, *we* thrive and flourish, but our own flourishing is meant to be *shared* with others. When we relate God's love only to our own personal need for righteousness, peace, and joy, the result ends up being like a spiritualized narcissism that is ultimately unfruitful. But as God's love *takes hold* of us on the inside, the result will be a much healthier approach to life, as we allow His love to propel us into a lifestyle of giving out and serving others.

Sadly, the devil has many of us convinced that our lives are too insignificant to make a difference.

Walking in love, we grow in fulfilling our purpose to reflect God's glory to a hurting and needy world. Remember, we are created in God's image. As such, we find our *deepest* joy and fulfillment in giving out and blessing others. Of course, this is where *grace* comes into the picture. Grace both inspires and enables us to live beyond ourselves. Grace enables us to live a life of giving that is *beyond reason.*

GOD WANTS TO USE *ME?*

Every day, as we interact with people, we will likely encounter need. The question is, do we live life with our *eyes open* to this? God's *grace* equips us to make a difference in the lives of people in need. It begins with *seeing* others through the eyes of His love and *responding* to needs in ways that can be small or great.

Sadly, the devil has many of us convinced that our lives are too insignificant to make a difference. We think, "Who am I to impact someone *else's* life? After all, I have problems of my own. I don't have the answers for my *own* life, much less someone else's. Until I have it all together myself, I'm not in a position to impact anyone else." This is a demonic lie that we cannot allow ourselves to believe.

None of us will *ever* have it "all together" in this life. Thus, if we think that way, we are setting ourselves up for a life that will bear very little fruit. The key to overcoming this lie is, once again, recognizing the nature of God's *unreasonable* grace. Just as God's grace *blesses* us beyond reason, His grace also *works through* us beyond reason. While it might not make sense to *you and me* that God would use us, that is exactly His intent. The consistent testimony of Scripture is that God uses flawed human beings to accomplish His purposes for blessing and redeeming the world. That is why *everyone* needs grace to live a fruitful life that blesses others. There are no exceptions.

Often, we might think that the people with the greatest impact on others are those who are most *gifted* or those blessed with the most *resources*. Scripture shows us otherwise. Consider Paul's words to the community in Corinth: "And God is able to make all grace overflow *to you*, so that by always having enough of everything, *you may overflow* in every good work" (2 Cor. 9:8, italics added). For you and me to live fruitful lives and *overflow* in acts of blessing to others, the most important key is *grace*, not gifting or resources. Many people possess much but do very little with it. But others, with modest gifting or possessions, *do* something with the little they have. God in His grace will *multiply* that, using it beyond its *apparent* value. Remember, grace will take us *beyond* what makes sense.

Perhaps this is why Yeshua made a point of noting the poor widow in Mark 12. She put into the offering an amount worth less than a penny, and those two coins were all she had. But

Yeshua said that in giving "out of her poverty..." (v. 44), her giving exceeded the larger contributions of the wealthy. How could this be? Because Yeshua was not referring to the *amount* she gave but the spirit in which she gave it. It was a gift of *faith*, an act of *worship*, enabled by *grace*. As such, her gift had a greater impact than what makes sense. Remember, it's by faith that we *enter into* the realm of God's grace.

In reading this passage recently, it struck me that when the widow came to give her offering, Yeshua did *not discourage* her from giving. That would have been *reasonable*, in light of her poverty. But Yeshua did not tell her to *hold onto* her coins. I suspect He wanted His disciples (and us) to see two key principles here:

1. Regardless of our status in life, we are created to be generous givers. Giving is part of our nature, and as such, our acts of giving express a foundational need and desire of the human heart.
2. The importance of our giving is not based on the size of what we can give, but rather, the faith seen in our willingness to give, even when our resources seem minimal.

We must see that our "gift" is never limited by its size. In other words, we should never judge our capacity for *blessing* others by looking at how *much* we are able to do or give. Grace multiplies what is done in faith, making it of greater value and impact than what is reasonable. To state this in different wording, we cannot *calculate* the true Kingdom value and impact of faith-filled giving and serving. Grace takes our acts of blessing *beyond reason*.

EVIDENCE OF A TRANSFORMED LIFE

At the core of a grace-filled walk of giving and serving are a transformed *heart* and life. But what might this *look* like? On the most basic level, God's work of transformation is seen as we experience freedom from bondage to *self*-centeredness, and we find ourselves living to give and to bless *others*. This is not a *total* change that happens suddenly, but one that takes place over the *process* of God working in our hearts. This is to be a *life orientation*, in which we embrace the values of God's Kingdom, and we rise above the *self-centered* ways so rooted in our culture and world. Giving and blessing are not simply actions that we do. They actually express our new *nature*, central to our identity as a Kingdom people.

God has given a deposit of *His own life* into us as believers. The Holy Spirit dwells in us, and yes, He is the great Comforter and Encourager, but He is so much more than that. His life in us is a *dynamic* life, meant for inspiring and empowering us for giving to others. Many believers seem to have little or no faith and vision for a life of giving. I believe such a lack of vision is due to deception as well as ignorance. The enemy seeks to deceive us into thinking that we have nothing to give—nothing by which we can bless others.

The deception is based largely on not understanding this work of God's grace in us. One of the devil's strategies is to keep us *self*-absorbed, bottling up this dynamic life of the Spirit. The temptation is for us to spend much time and energy focusing on *our problems* and how to get them solved. Certainly there is a place for giving attention to our problems, but in our culture today, we often take this to an extreme.

A key message of Scripture is that we find our deepest sense of meaning and purpose as we are *giving* to others. This is a Kingdom value that stands in contrast to the self-absorbed ways of worldly thinking. Our culture today is driven by principles of pride, lust, greed, and natural reasoning. God's Kingdom is driven by love, humility, serving, giving, and faith. It is with this in view that Paul exhorted the believers in Corinth to "excel" in the "grace" of giving (see 2 Corinthians 8:7).

For us as believers, at the heart of the giving lifestyle to which we are called, is the knowledge that God has given His Spirit to each of us. It is the presence of the Spirit that empowers us for a life in which we *partner with* God in seeing His blessing touch others *through us*. His *grace* is what makes this "partnership" both possible and powerful.

INTERCESSORY LIVES

There is a phrase I believe is appropriate in characterizing the life we are called to live. We are to live in what I call an *intercessory* mentality or an intercessory lifestyle. Typically, we use the word "intercession" in relation to *prayer*, but we can gain some insight by considering a broader meaning of the word. In the Hebrew Bible, the word often used for "intercede" is the Hebrew root *pahgah*. In some of its usage, it means to come upon or encounter, with the idea of *making contact*. I think we could say that Yeshua was the ultimate example of one who *lived* an intercessory life. Certainly in laying down His life at the cross, Yeshua interceded for humanity.

Time after time, we see accounts of Yeshua looking upon multitudes of people who were hurting, and His response was to connect with their lives and needs.

I think we could say His entire *life* on this Earth was an intercessory life. Yeshua saw the *need* of humanity, and He *responded* to that need by stepping down from the realm of glory into the condition of our humanness. Yeshua placed Himself *into* our human experience. But of course, unlike us, He never sinned.

We could also say that the *manner* in which Yeshua lived out His life and ministry was intercessory. What do I mean by that? Simply that Yeshua did not *distance* Himself from the lives and needs of people. Time after time, we see accounts of Yeshua looking upon multitudes of people who were hurting, and His response was to *connect* with their lives and needs. He reached out to them, knowing that He *had* what was needed for impacting their lives with the power and presence of God. The prophet Isaiah wrote prophetically of the Messiah to come. His description captures this intercessory life and ministry of Yeshua, who quoted this passage, clearly applying it to Himself:

The Spirit of Adonai Elohim is on me, because Adonai has anointed me to proclaim Good News to the poor. He has sent me to bind up the brokenhearted, to proclaim liberty to the captives and the opening of the prison to those who are bound...to console those who mourn in Zion, to give them beauty for ashes, the oil of joy for mourning, the garment of praise for the spirit of heaviness, that they might be called oaks of righteousness, the planting of Adonai, that He may be glorified (Isaiah 61:1–3).

With Yeshua as our example, we are to embrace a mindset in which we live with a *readiness* to give as we see people's needs. That does not mean that *you and I* are to fully *meet* their needs. It does mean we live with an openness to God *using* us to *take part* in meeting their needs. When we live in that mentality and respond to need, we can see the unlimited potential of God's grace working through us to bless others. This intercessory life arises from our ongoing walk of *relationship* with the Lord, and from that relationship, we *connect* with the lives of others.

But it is also important for us to understand some foundational Kingdom principles, helping us to see how we can participate in this intercessory life.

THE SEED OF GOD'S LIFE

We can gain some insight as we consider the writing of Peter from his first letter:

Love one another fervently with a pure heart, having been born again, not of corruptible seed but incorruptible, through the word of God which lives and abides forever (1 Peter 1:22b–23, NKJV, italics added).

Therefore, *laying aside* all malice, all deceit, hypocrisy, envy, and all evil speaking, as newborn babes, desire the pure milk of the word, that you may grow thereby, if indeed *you have tasted* that the Lord is gracious (1 Peter 2:1–3, NKJV, italics added).

Peter is writing here to encourage his readers to love one another. He is telling us that we have the *capacity* to love, because we have been born again and given the "incorruptible seed" of God's eternal Word. There is a flow of life from God's heart to ours. That flow is pure and life giving, imparting grace to us for loving and blessing others beyond what comes naturally to us.

> *God's Word and His Spirit bring about a washing in our hearts, enabling us to love from a "pure heart."*

God's Word and His Spirit bring about a washing in our hearts, enabling us to love from a "pure heart." The word "pure" here does not suggest perfection, but more the idea of a heart that is clean or clear. In other words, it is a heart that is not "cluttered" with carnal attitudes of malice, envy, and evil speaking. Such ways are self-centered, and as such, they are like pollutants in the "environment" of our hearts. They interfere with the flow of God's life *to us* and also *from* us to others. So Peter exhorts us to *lay aside* or put away self-serving attitudes. They hinder our capacity for loving and blessing others. Just as we ourselves have experienced a "taste" of God's graciousness, we want to *impart* grace as well.

We all are likely *aware* of the presence of self-centeredness in our lives. I am not suggesting we must be totally free from all traces of self-centeredness before God can use us. But I do believe that if we want to grow in our walk with God, we must take steps to *deal* with self-centered attitudes and ways. Of course, in our flesh, our preference would be that *God* would just "take care of it" *for* us and sweep away all traces of selfishness from us. We would love for Him to just sovereignly *take away* our self-centeredness, without us having to make any changes ourselves. But while God has given us, in Messiah, a new spirit, He also gives *us* the responsibility for changing our attitudes and ways. Yes, He helps us with this and empowers us for it, but such change involves *choices* we must make in the course of life—choices that are key to releasing the grace we need for Spirit-empowered change.

A BEGINNING POINT

How is it, then, that we can lay aside those ways that are rooted in self-centeredness? I believe we can see helpful keys in the twelfth chapter of Paul's letter to the believers in Rome. Much of the chapter is relevant, but our focus will just be on two verses.

First, consider verse 9, which says, "Let love be without hypocrisy—detesting what is evil, holding fast to the good." This identifies for us a beginning point—a foundational *attitude* we are to embrace. Laying aside self-centeredness *begins* with a basic heart stance of sincerely hating and rejecting self-centeredness and clinging to graciousness and all that it implies. I know that sounds simplistic, but let's consider an application.

In Psalm 139, David made a request of the Lord that is certainly relevant to us as New Covenant believers. He prayed, "Search me, O God, and know my heart! Try me, and know my thoughts! And see if there be any grievous way in me, and lead me in the way everlasting!" (Ps. 139:23–24, ESV). The prophet, Jeremiah, wrote of the human heart as being "deceitful above all things…" (Jere. 17:9).

David, in spite of his love for God, recognized within himself the potential for his own heart to be deceived. He was even referred to as "a man after (God's) own heart" (1 Sam. 13:14), but he recognized the capacity of his own heart to go astray. Thus, he invited the Lord to search his heart and examine him for offensive ways. He *wanted to know* if any of his attitudes differed from the way God Himself sees things. At the heart of this desire was a love for righteousness and a sincere hatred of evil and sin. Again, this does not suggest a *perfectly lived* life, but it does suggest a *sincerely devoted* life, committed to God's ways.

We can truly love God, yet we may still tolerate attitudes that can lead us astray. In my own prayer life, I regularly ask God to search my own heart. I regularly ask Him to give me a holy hatred for sin and compromise and a love for His correction. I want to see things His way, not my own. I fully understand that I am a new creation in Yeshua, and He has imparted to me His perfect righteousness. But I still am aware of the capacity of my own heart to be deceived and drawn away. Thus, I ask the Lord for His searching and revealing of my heart so that I can stay on track with Him. I want to see people the way He sees them and love the way He loves.

With these thoughts in mind, we can pray regularly for God to search our own hearts in relation to self-centered ways. A simple example might be: "Lord, would you open my heart to see any ways I have tolerated malice, deceit, hypocrisy, envy, or evil speaking? Have I allowed anger or jealousy to have a place in my heart? Have I been blind to any of these ways in my own life? Give me a hatred for ways that are not in line with Your love. Help me to detest what is evil and hold fast to what is good so that my heart will be a reflection of Your gracious heart. Help me recognize anything in me that interferes with Your love."

We want our eyes to be open to attitudes and ways that hinder the flow of God's love through us. Thus, we can pray for the "searchlight" of God's Spirit to open our eyes to ways we need to grow. Once again, this is not for the purpose of condemnation, but rather for growing in vision for how our lives can become more like Yeshua. Such an attitude marks a *beginning* point for identifying and laying aside self-centered ways.

OVERCOMING EVIL WITH GOOD

Coming back to Romans 12, Paul follows verse 9 with a series of exhortations related to attitudes and actions that show us what radical love might look like. He touches on behavior that, honestly, can be so challenging to the ways and reactions that often come naturally to us. We are instructed to *bless* those who treat us wrongly, to *never* do evil in return for evil done to us, to never seek revenge. Then he concludes the passage with a summary statement that, once again, seems almost too simplistic: "Do not be overcome by evil, but overcome evil with good" (Rom. 12:21). Far from being simplistic, this exhortation represents a powerful principle, describing an aspect of *spiritual warfare* in which we are to participate.

What Paul is talking about here is the idea of bringing the Spirit of Yeshua into situations in which we have experienced some level of mistreatment by others. The natural response when mistreated is to *react* to the person who mistreated us. We are tempted to retaliate, or at least to hold a grudge and consider the opportunity for vengeance. Paul is saying that if we react in such ways, we are simply continuing in the same spirit as the wrong that was done *to us*. We are perpetuating the evil, and as such, we have allowed it to "overcome" or conquer us.

How do we overcome evil? We overcome it by responding in the opposite spirit.

When we react to evil in the same spirit as what is done to us, we are giving evil the victory over us in that situation. We are not overcome by evil simply by having *experienced* mistreatment. Evil can overcome us only if *we allow* mistreatment to draw us into the same spirit. How do *we* overcome evil? We overcome it by responding in the opposite spirit. Paul wants us to see that grace from God is available to us for *responding* in the Spirit of Yeshua rather than *reacting* in the flesh. There is *grace* for us to do what is unreasonable as we love and bless rather than react with retaliation.

Let's relate this *principle* to laying aside self-centered ways. We defeat selfishness in ourselves by taking *steps of action* that *override* selfishness. Acts of giving and blessing have a powerful impact to override selfishness in us. Giving to someone becomes our step of faith in which we lay aside self-centeredness so that God's Spirit can then bless and *anoint* our act of giving in redemptive ways. Once we recognize in ourselves attitudes and ways rooted in self-centeredness ("Search me O

God…"), we realize that situations in which we are tempted to react carnally are actually opportunities to *lay aside* carnal ways that tempt us.

Once again, our preference in this regard is that God would just sweep selfishness out of our hearts, but God puts the victory in *our* hands. He instructs *us* to *lay aside,* or defeat, the selfishness by *blessing* the very one against whom we are tempted to react.

The point is, for some areas of spiritual warfare, we *pray* our way through to the victory. But this is an area in which the victory comes as we *act* in love, even though we may not feel like doing so. The result will be an inward victory in which the grip of self-centeredness becomes weakened. We learn to "lay aside" the different *ungracious* attitudes and ways that come naturally to us as we draw on God's grace for overcoming evil with good.

For example, if someone sins against us, our natural reaction is to become offended. But rather than allowing offense, we choose to forgive the offender. However, we can sometimes find that even as we forgive, the feelings of offense or hurt might remain. Overcoming evil with good takes us beyond merely forgiving as we look for ways we can actually *bless* the one who offended us. On the most basic level, we can do this by sincerely praying for the offender and asking God to bless him or her. But we can also look for practical ways to bless.

Our feelings of offense and the *urge* to retaliate are overcome as we actively bless those who may sin against us. The act of blessing becomes a step of spiritual warfare that brings inward freedom to us. Now, we will likely have to repeat such faith actions *many times* in our lives. Unloving or ungracious attitudes do not usually disappear permanently after one instance of overcoming evil with good. But I think you will find that, in each instance, you are weakening the intensity of the inward grip of self-centeredness, and over time, acts of love and blessing become more natural to you.

When we sense the Spirit leading us to give or bless, but we also feel an inward tug to hold back, we don't have to feel powerless against that pull of self-centeredness. The seed of Yeshua's life is in us. Thus, we can be confident that, if we will step out from the place of guardedness and self-centeredness into generosity and blessing, God's grace will meet us and release inward joy, as well as empowerment for the acts of giving.

God is calling us to leave self-centered living behind.

MISUNDERSTANDING GOD'S ANOINTING

Let's come back to Peter's exhortation, quoted earlier, to love others from a pure or clean heart. Remember, Peter was instructing us to lay aside self-centered ways that keep us from growing as people of love. As the Spirit of God opens our eyes to opportunities for blessing others, we are to resist the pull of selfishness and step out in *faith* to give and bless. But beyond self-centeredness, there are misconceptions we can have about God's ways as He chooses to use us for bringing blessing.

Sometimes we want to *feel* some kind of anointing or overwhelming stirring in us before we will take actions of faith. We can think, "Lord, anoint me so I can step out and be a blessing to others." On one hand, there is a *right* desire here to not want to step out in the flesh or our natural human ability. But such thinking misses something about how God's Spirit seems to work. I believe God wants us to step out in *faith*, in response to the Spirit's prompting or conviction, before we may *feel* any sense of His pleasure, anointing, or power. We prefer *feeling* something first because that will give us more confidence for embracing the *risk* involved in our steps of faith.

But the biblical pattern is that the *anointing* of God *follows* actions of faith and obedience. We will experience God's joy and pleasure as we, through our faith-obedience, submit our lives to *actions* of giving. Why? Because, in giving, we are yielding our *hearts* to the spirit of generosity. As we step out in faith to bless others, we are functioning as God intends for us to function, and we *feel His pleasure* in that.

First, we step out in the natural realm, in response to an inward sense to help or bless someone. There may be little or no *feeling* of anointing or blessing, but as we sense a prompting in our hearts, we respond to it, even if it seems unreasonable.

When we *do respond,* the Spirit of God releases His joy and pleasure and freedom, amid our *actions* of giving.

Too often, people are waiting to *feel* inspired to give or to *feel* empowered. But I believe we will *feel* inspired and empowered as we obey. Our *obedience,* which becomes the expression of our *faith,* leads us into God's joy and empowerment. Remember, it is *by faith* that we can *enter into* God's grace and empowerment (see Romans 5:2).

THE POWER OF A SEED

Yeshua's own teaching can give us some further insight on this issue from a different perspective. Instructing His disciples about the nature of God's Kingdom, Yeshua frequently referred to *seeds* as giving a picture of how God's Kingdom works. Consider one such teaching, or parable, from Mark 4:

> Then He said, "To what shall we liken the kingdom of God? Or with what parable shall we picture it? It is like a mustard seed which, when it is sown on the ground, is smaller than all the seeds on earth; but when it is sown, it grows up and becomes greater than all herbs, and shoots out large branches, so that the birds of the air may nest under its shade" (Mark 4:30–32, NKJV).

The life of God Himself has been sown as a seed in our hearts. It began as something small, a tiny seed planted in us when we first put our faith in Yeshua. Thus, while our lives *were* carnal and self-centered, we now have the seed of *Yeshua's life* within us. We are to see, with eyes of faith, that there is mighty power in that tiny seed. If we will give the seed room to grow, then, like the mustard seed, it will grow increasingly larger inside us.

The key is, we *give* ourselves to the *process* of obedience, embracing a *lifestyle* of giving and selflessness. That obedience clears from our hearts more and more of the "weeds" and "debris." Our obedience allows for the implanted seed to grow and consume more and more of our inner being. As the seed grows, we experience increasing freedom in giving to others. We encounter less inward resistance as God's life and nature *grows* inside us.

The growth takes place as we step out purely in faith-obedience, at a point when there is no great sense of anointing or *feeling* the Spirit's presence. It often begins with just a subtle prompting in our hearts, based on awareness of a need we could help meet. So we step out in obedience into a place where God's Spirit is given greater freedom to work, both *in* our hearts and *through* our actions.

> *The key is, we give ourselves to the process of obedience, embracing a lifestyle of giving and selflessness.*

As believers, we want to experience the supernatural work of the Holy Spirit to lift us up into something greater than our own natural ability. We need to step off the shore into the deeper waters of faith if we want to be used by the Spirit. You see, the "shore" is the place of comfort and no risk. It represents the values of just surviving and living self-centered lives. We must get *away* from the shore if we want to get *into* fruitful life in the Spirit.

Think about watching someone surfing. Does the wave come to the shore and just pick up the surfer and carry him or her out to the deeper waters? Of course not! Like the surfer, *we* are to step away from the shore to *get to* the wave, which is symbolic of the anointing of the Spirit. That is the nature of this aspect of our walk in the Spirit. We are to *give* ourselves over to unselfish thinking rooted in faith and compassion. In other words, we must *move toward* needs rather than distancing ourselves from them.

Look for people with needs—situations in which your time, energy, possessions, and spiritual gifts can bless others. *Look* for opportunities requiring faith. As you give yourself to those opportunities, you will see joy as well as anointing flow increasingly in your life. Don't wait for the joy and anointing to come *first*. Rather, step out in faith, even when it is uncomfortable to do so—that is the point where God meets us.

WHEN THE SEED IS *SOWN*

There is another misconception that holds people back from giving. I suspect this is something many struggle with. Sometimes, we can feel intimidated by the *size* of the need we encounter. Let's consider a simple example of receiving a fund-raising letter from a worthy ministry. We read of the ministry's need for a million dollars for a special project, but as we consider our own finances, we have only a small gift we could give. We might think something like, "The need is so great that I can't see how *I* can even make a dent on it. I don't see how the little I may have could make any difference." Thus, we hold back from giving because the size of the need has left us concluding that our small gift is of little value.

This is just one type of example, involving finances, but it shows how we can allow ourselves to feel overwhelmed by the *size* of needs we might encounter, and we shrink back from giving to a situation of need.

Grace multiplies what is done in faith, making it of greater value and impact than what is reasonable.

We must remember what we concluded earlier in the chapter, when considering Yeshua's emphasis on a poor widow's giving. We saw that we should not judge our capacity for blessing others by looking at how *much* we are able to do or give. We must see that *grace multiplies* what is done in faith, making it of greater value and impact than what is reasonable.

With that in mind, let's come back to Yeshua's sharing on the *seed*, and we can gain further insight into the principle here. Go back a few pages and reread Yeshua's parable of the mustard seed, but read it with a slightly different interpretation. Consider the mustard seed as seed that *we sow* in any number of contexts of life.

It could be the context of sharing a simple word of encouragement with someone who is hurting, or giving to help meet a financial need we are aware of. It could be sharing the Good News of Messiah with someone else, praying for the sick, or expressing our spiritual gifting in some way. It is seed that *we sow* as we give in some way to someone else.

What we have to give, in and of itself, may be small or appear insignificant, like the mustard seed. But *like* that seed Yeshua spoke of, there is dynamic Kingdom power within it. When we hold back, due to feeling like we cannot really make a difference, we are not recognizing the *supernatural* nature of the Kingdom and the nature of the *seed* we are sowing in faith.

Consider Yeshua's words about the mustard seed. He said that at the point when the seed is sown, it is the smallest of seeds. But *when* the mustard seed *is sown*, that marks a beginning point of a transformation process in which the tiny seed *grows into* something greater than the others.

This is so simple that we can miss the point here. *When* it is sown, it *grows*. If it is *not* sown, nothing will happen. When we lean on natural reasoning to talk ourselves out of acts of giving and blessing, concluding that our gift is too insignificant to make any difference, we are discounting the supernatural nature of God's Kingdom. Yeshua likened it to the transformation that takes place with a seed that is sown. What the seed *becomes* does not even resemble what it looked like before it was sown.

God does not promise to multiply the seed we hold onto. But He does multiply seed we are willing to sow. What that means is, however little we think we have to offer in a situation of need, if the Lord prompts us, and we *sow in faith*, He will *multiply* it. We need to be willing to *believe* this because it will impact how God will use us if we are willing to take the risks of faith. This is the nature of God's grace. It will take us *beyond reason*.

We cannot lose sight of this liberating truth. Losing sight of this leaves so many believers feeling like we have little to give or offer for blessing others. But *seeing* this truth will lead us to expect God to do something far beyond what is reasonable with our small "seed." But we do have to be willing to *sow* it at the point when it *looks* insignificant. We must be willing to step out in faith for God to use us to bless others. This is part of what it means to step outside our "comfort zone."

Paul communicates similarly in 2 Corinthians 9:10: "Now may He who supplies seed to the sower, and bread for food, supply and *multiply* the seed *you have sown* and increase the fruits of your righteousness" (NKJV, italics added). Again, God does not multiply what we hold onto; He multiplies what we sow. If you encounter what appears to be an impossible need, don't shrink back, assuming that what you *have* does not appear to even begin to meet the need. If the Spirit prompts you, step out and *sow the seed*, and believe *God will multiply* it in the ground where it is sown.

It has nothing to do with the size of the seed and everything to do with our willingness to believe and respond. We must see that Yeshua *expects* this of us. This is *why* He gave us the different parables that describe the nature of God's Kingdom working in us and through us.

Do you recall the times when Yeshua and His disciples were among crowds of thousands of hungry people? The disciples discussed among themselves what they should do. Should they send the people away? Should they go into the village to try to come up with food to feed the people? Feeding a crowd this size would be impossible based on the resources.

But during their discussion, Yeshua says, "They (the crowd) don't need to leave—*you give them* something to eat" (Matt. 14:16, italics added). The idea was to get whatever little they had and feed the people. Of course, what Yeshua was telling them to do *made no sense*. But someone realized that there was a boy with a small amount of fish and bread, and Yeshua *multiplied* that to feed thousands. Later, they were picking up the leftovers.

I believe Yeshua wanted to stir something in the disciples, giving them a sense of vision for *grace*-filled supernatural giving—giving and seeing *God multiply* the seed that is sown. He was planting in them a mindset that would no longer think in terms of lack or "What do *I* have to give that could make any difference?" Rather, He wanted them to see that, "*If* I will *give* what I *do have*, and I give it in faith, God will multiply it." He wanted them to see that there is always miraculous potential when faith and obedience come together in situations that appear impossible.

God's grace, met with *our faith*, will multiply a *little* to accomplish much!

NO APOLOGY NEEDED

When encountering a situation of need, have you ever found yourself apologizing for the "smallness" of what you had to offer? Whatever the situation might be—whether it's giving money, your talents and abilities, or your prayers or words of encouragement—whatever is called for, no apology is needed! When we reach out to help someone, but we qualify it with the apology, "I'm sorry, I wish I could do more, but this is all I can do...," we are minimizing the Kingdom impact of our "gift." By apologizing for the "smallness" of what we have to offer, we are essentially declaring that we *don't have faith* for our gift to be of any value to someone in need. We are suggesting that if we had more to give, it could *then* be meaningful.

When we do this, it reveals that we are thinking on a purely natural level, thus, leaving God out of the picture. We are thinking that the value lies in the *size* of what we give rather than in the supernatural nature of the *Kingdom* in which we participate. Remember, the value of our "offering" is never based on its size, but rather on the power of *God* to *multiply* our offering into something far more than what is reasonable. You see, too often we can buy into what I would call "the deception of insufficiency" or the deception of our personal insignificance.

I'm certainly not suggesting we should see ourselves in a prideful way. But we *are* to see that God's grace empowers us to make a difference in the lives of others. We fully understand that apart from God's help, we can do nothing of Kingdom value. But to see ourselves as too *insignificant* to be used by God is really just a form of false humility. Grace imparts a godly significance to our lives as we participate, by faith, in a life that is far more fruitful than anything we could have imagined.

DON'T BELIEVE THE LIE!

This is one reason for the enemy's strategy to weigh us down with sin, condemnation, shame, discouragement, fear, hopelessness, and more. When weighed down in such ways, we will be blind to the possibilities of a fruitful life of giving to bless others. We will remain "on the shore" rather than stepping out into deeper waters of faith. The demonic lie of our personal insignificance is meant to leave us concluding that we have nothing to offer for the benefit of others. Believing this lie leaves us feeling like we personally have no value to God or anyone else. If we think this way, we will not likely respond to opportunities to give and bless.

This creates a serious problem because a basic aspect of our makeup as human beings is that we experience our highest sense of purpose and fulfillment in *giving* to bless others. I am *not* suggesting that we find our sense of personal worth in achievement. I'm simply saying that the lifestyle of serving and giving, for the benefit of others, is where we find joy and fulfillment on the deepest levels.

> **A basic aspect of our makeup as human beings is that we experience our highest sense of purpose and fulfillment in giving to bless others.**

With that in mind, we can see how demonic it is that the devil has so many people trapped in bondage to self-centered living. He also has many trapped in bondage to a *poverty mentality* that wrongly assumes that, because someone has *little* to give, then they cannot be givers at all. This is truly a demonic lie because when we feel we have nothing to give, we end up feeling humiliated and ashamed. That is exactly where the enemy wants to keep us, as he seeks to rob us of a personal sense of dignity. This leaves human beings, for whom God Himself has love and compassion, feeling instead like we have no sense of value or purpose.

Again, I am not referring here to a prideful sense of self-importance. I am speaking of a godly sense of dignity. This is the kind of dignity that David expressed in Psalm 139, where he declares to the Lord, "I praise You, for I am awesomely, wonderfully made! Wonderful are Your works—and my soul knows that very well" (Ps. 139:14). Keep in mind that, when he refers to God's "works" as "wonderful," he is talking about *himself*! Is David being prideful or egotistical? No, he is simply recognizing that, as a creation of God, his life (and every human life) displays the wonder and glory of God's brilliance.

If we believe the lie of our worthlessness or insignificance, we will almost certainly rule out the possibility of living a fruitful life that blesses others. This is why we must see that the issue is never how *much* we have to give. The issue is, are we willing to *do something* with what we *do have*? Everyone has *something* to give to bless others. Remember, natural reasoning—especially worldly thinking—reverses God's order.

With worldly thinking, we gain a sense of value in what we *possess* and what we *accumulate*. Of course, there is no blessing on the reversing of God's order, so many *accumulate* much yet still feel unfulfilled. Why? Because God's blessing is not on what we accumulate; the blessing is on what we give away. That is why the person who has little does not have to feel a loss of dignity or purpose. Giving from what we do have is what releases the blessing, joy, and fulfillment in us and through us.

As you encounter people and situations of great need, don't shrink back or feel overwhelmed. Give what *you* can give, and believe God will multiply *your* seed that is sown. Maybe *you* don't have enough to meet the need, but *God does*, and once *you* sow what *you have*, you are giving God something to *multiply* to meet the need. How does God do that? You don't really have to know the answer to that. He can bring in others alongside you to join in, and they end up picking up the need with you.

Your simple obedience to give what might appear insignificant can set in motion a release of *God's* abundance to meet the rest of the need. Remember, this whole issue of giving to others is not about *me* being able to *fully meet* the other person's need. It's about me, *partnering with God,* as *He* meets the need, and uses me as a part of the process. Our partnering with God—our willingness to sow the seed we have—releases God's grace and supply into the situation.

The bottom line is, this is a *supernatural* life we are part of as followers of Yeshua. Don't try to calculate it and figure it all out using logic and common sense. Obviously, there *is* a place for that, but logic and common sense cannot be the basis for assessing the *Kingdom* value of a life of giving and blessing. God's unreasonable grace makes it possible for you and me to impact others in ways that do not make sense. Faith and love become the keys to our access into this grace. God's call on our lives is not to merely survive, but to live beyond ourselves, as we live to reveal His love and nature to those around us.

Chapter Thirteen

DAY BY DAY

Our journey into the realm of "grace beyond reason" has led us to consider some foundational areas in which God's grace impacts us. As important as it is to *learn* of these basic aspects of the work of grace, we must also embrace the challenge of *applying* grace in our daily lives.

I have noted in every chapter that because grace is so far beyond reason, we can struggle to fully comprehend the glorious nature of the life into which grace leads us. It is such a challenge for us to see how it is possible for God, who is infinite in His perfection, to bridge the massive "gap" between Himself and us. But that is exactly what God has done for us through Yeshua. Grace is what makes this impossible task a possibility.

The question we are left with is this: Will we embrace the *faith challenge* of entering this realm of God's unreasonable grace? We must recognize that our "entering in" to grace is not just a one-time event that takes place when we first receive Messiah. Day by day, and perhaps numerous times in a day, we must consciously refocus our attention on who God is and what He has done, and continues to do, in our lives. The daily battle we face is ultimately to get our eyes off of ourselves and

165

onto Yeshua. Otherwise, grace will just remain to us an inspiring *idea* with little or no substance.

IT'S ALL ABOUT *HIM*

The mistake that can tempt us all is to think that our performance—the successes and failures of our spiritual lives—determines our potential for Kingdom fruitfulness. But our performance is *not* what determines this. Yes, it helps us assess our progress and identify where change is needed. But our *performance* is not the gauge for determining our potential for fruitful lives. The determining factor is God's unreasonable grace, through which we gain access to a life in which limitations and impossibilities are overcome.

> *Our shortcomings do not have to limit us. It is our shortcomings that inform us of our need for grace.*

The problem is, we tend to see grace as being *limited* by our performance. In other words, we see the shortcomings in our walk with God, and we can get frustrated with ourselves, concluding that our lives are too flawed for God to use us. But the reality is, our shortcomings do not have to limit us. It is our shortcomings that *inform* us of our *need* for grace. When this recognition is combined with repentance and faith, we can begin to see the progress we desire in our walk with God. But we must remind ourselves daily that grace is all about *God* and who *He* is, not about *us* and how well *we are doing*. To the degree that our focus is on ourselves and our performance, we will be unable to gain access to grace. Grace defies logic and natural reasoning. That is why we can only enter it *by faith*.

At the risk of sounding overly simplistic, let me repeat this basic truth: The daily battle we face is to get our focus off ourselves and onto the Lord. The degree to which we *win that battle* will determine how far we will go in His grace, as we seek to walk out God's call and destiny for our lives.

THE TRAP OF "WORKS RIGHTEOUSNESS"

While we can know with certainty that our own good works do not earn us anything in our walk with God, we still must be alert to the traps of *works righteousness*. In our desire to live a life pleasing to the Lord, I suspect we all have tendencies to slip into various forms of works righteousness, which usually leads to a mindset of *striving*.

When I speak of "works righteousness" I am referring to the tendency to feel good or bad about our "value" to God based on our performance. We can fully understand that our *forgiveness* is based on *Yeshua's* perfect righteousness. Yet we still can feel like *our behavior* is what determines how God sees us and "feels" about us. We can truly desire to please God and honor Him in how we live, yet we grow frustrated with our tendency to fall short. We then assume *God* must be frustrated with us as well. God does not "write us off" and give up on us if He sees that we are not measuring up. Certainly we all should *want* to be a people who are wholehearted in loving God and serving Him with our lives. But the works-righteousness mindset leaves us just *trying* so hard, *striving* to do everything just right.

We must see that if we are *striving*, then we are not *trusting*. So then, what is it we are to be putting our trust in? We put our trust in the *faithfulness and sufficiency* of God Himself.

Over the years, I have been inspired and challenged by reading biographies of godly believers from past generations. One such biography is focused on the life of James Hudson Taylor, founder of the China Inland Mission. Taylor had a groundbreaking and fruitful ministry in China, beginning in the mid-1800s and continuing for decades. He was passionate in his commitment to the Lord and his zeal for serving Him. But he often grew disheartened as he saw his own imperfections.

In the book *Hudson Taylor's Spiritual Secret*, the author describes some of the ups and downs Taylor would go through. One day, he would feel very zealous and a strong sense of God's presence, but the next day, he would feel pulled and tossed by temptation. This would leave him feeling distant from God, wondering if his faith was even genuine. This was at a time in his life when he was already involved in full-time missions. He was not in rebellion or living a self-centered life, but he struggled with seeing his imperfections as he sought to live out the high standards of God's Word. He would often feel despair because his flaws were prominent in his thinking.

Again, such focus leads to striving, a mindset of *trying harder* in our own strength to feel pleasing to God. It was a stumbling block for Taylor until God gave him a simple revelation that became a key to life-changing victory in his walk. He came to see the importance of *resting* in what *God* has done rather than *striving* to try to *feel* faithful and zealous. This was not just an intellectual idea but part of a life-changing encounter with God's Spirit. God's *grace* became his primary focus and source of identity, rather than his own shortcomings. The following words, which Taylor wrote after his breakthrough, are simple, yet profound:

> Once I used to *try* to think very much and very often about Jesus, but *I often forgot Him.* Now I *trust Jesus* to *keep* my heart remembering Him, and *He does so*[1] (italics added).

Can you relate to what he shares here? I know *I* can relate to it. How often might we experience the frustration, and even the guilt, of *desiring* to keep our focus on the Lord, yet often forgetting Him and falling short of our desires? But with the help of God's Spirit, Hudson Taylor took hold of this revelation of not *striving* but *trusting* in *God's faithfulness.* Again, this can sound so simple that we miss the practicality and freedom in what he is saying.

Let me give an example. In our interaction with the Lord, as we express our commitment to Him, we might say something like, "Lord, I really want to serve You with my life. I want to be used by You and live for You totally." Then we may

---

1 Dr. and Mrs. Howard Taylor, *Hudson Taylor's Spiritual Secret* (Chicago: Moody Press, 1989), 178.

stumble in some way, and we begin to question whether our own sincerity is real.

Of course, the devil will also remind us of our unworthiness. He may whisper to us something like this: "You may *want* to serve God, but you know you're not good enough. You know you don't have enough faith…you don't pray enough…you're too self-centered…you have too many problems…" The enemy can present us with an endless list of past and present issues, attitudes, and sins, suggesting we must be disqualified from serving God on any level. Of course, we know that the devil is "the accuser" of believers (see Revelation 12:10), as well as a deceiver (see John 8:44). However, we still can get tripped up by such thoughts because there is usually some degree of accuracy to them. The enemy's suggestions of disqualification can seem believable to us because we are well aware of our shortcomings.

GOD IS NOT SURPRISED

At such times, we cannot allow ourselves to believe the enemy's lies. We must recognize that any *accuracy* in the accusations does not have to lead to the *conclusions* the enemy suggests. Our imperfections, while real, do not disqualify us.

Let's just use some common sense on this issue. God is not under any illusion that you or I can perfectly live out our life in Messiah. Yet He still has vision and destiny for us to be conformed to Yeshua's likeness and represent Him to those around us. That destiny is not contingent on us getting "our act" totally together. Rather, it is contingent on our being quick to respond to His correction, repent, and turn to Him at every point of need.

Remember, our life in God is all about *relationship*. It is the context of relationship in which we are empowered for the life and destiny into which we are called. Focusing on our flaws will leave us keeping ourselves at a distance from God rather than *turning to* Him. But God *invites* us to come to Him in our times of *need*, and he does not expect us to come into perfection first. His goal for us to be like Yeshua does not change just because He finds that we fall short. He is not shocked by our flaws. He knows we are *growing into* our likeness to His Son.

What we must do, at times when we are acutely aware of our flaws or the weakness of our faith, is go right back to the Lord. We must get our focus on Him and off ourselves. There is no empowerment for change apart from an ongoing *relationship* with Him. Thus, we *must* turn to the Lord, even in—especially in—those times when we *feel* we must be unwelcome.

The following is an example of how we might pray at such times:

> Lord, I *want* to be fully yielded to You, but I can see the ways I still hold myself back from full surrender. I can recognize the self-centeredness that often trips me up and different ways I still let You down. But Lord, I *look to You* and *trust* in You to work in me in every area where I see that *I lack.*

This type of prayer represents the stance of the one who recognizes that *Yeshua* is our *sufficiency.*

We cannot find the sufficiency in ourselves to serve Him adequately. If we try, we will discover that our flaws are what stand out most prominently to us, leaving us discouraged or even hopeless. We cannot try to *work up* a likeness to Yeshua. Yes, there are right choices we will face, moment by moment of each day, but becoming like Yeshua is a work of *His grace,* not *our striving.*

There is liberating grace in seeing the truth of Philippians 2:13: "For the One working in you is God—both to *will* and to *work* for His good pleasure" (italics added). This is such a powerful statement. Paul is telling us that God Himself will be our source, giving us the *heart* for serving Him (the *will*), as well as the *empowerment* for serving Him (the *work*). What a promise this is! Even at those times when our *will* to serve the Lord may be weak or lacking, He commits Himself to be at work in us, in *that specific area* of our weakness. He is promising to help us, even in the area of our *desire.*

I am *human*, and often *I feel* the weakness of my human nature as it affects my walk with God. There are times when *I feel* the weakness of my own faith, times when I am down instead of up, times when I *feel* more defeated than victorious, times when I *feel* unspiritual. I truly wish this never happened, but it does. Now, I'm not suggesting it is fine to just accept whatever moods come over us. When attacked with discouragement, hopelessness, or any other attitudes that seek to pull us down and get our focus on ourselves, we must *resist* those attitudes and fight against them.

But sometimes, I feel like the *fight* is just not there. Do you ever feel that way?

Again, I am not saying we should just accept such feelings and not resist them. I am simply saying that *feeling* the weakness of our human nature is normal for human beings. Our weakness does not disqualify us from God's calling or blessing, but we do need to *recognize* our weakness and look to God and His grace.

HELP MY UNBELIEF!

I am reminded of the account in Mark 9, where a man comes to Yeshua on behalf of his son, who is demonically oppressed. He asks Yeshua to have compassion for his son and help him. Yeshua answers, telling him, "All things are possible for one who believes!" (Mark 9:23).

The father responds, declaring, "I believe! Help my unbelief!" (Mark 9:24).

Yeshua then proceeds to cast out the demon and heal the man's son. There is an important principle to see in this account, especially in the exchange between Yeshua and the father. The principle is this: God does not require *per-*

God does not require perfect faith from us to do His redemptive works in our lives.

fect faith from us to do His redemptive works in our lives. To paraphrase the father in this particular encounter, I think he was saying, in essence, "Lord, I do believe, but I also recognize the *weakness* in my own faith. I am so aware of the unbelief warring against my ability to simply trust You. Would You 'help my unbelief'—meet me at my level of faith and supply what *I don't have*?" Yeshua did *exactly that*. He responded to the father's expressed "seed" of faith, and He proceeded to cast out the demon and heal the boy.

God meets us in our weakness and place of need. He doesn't require perfection from us in order to respond. He simply looks for us to recognize our lack and look to *Him* for what we don't have in ourselves. This can be such a helpful principle for receiving grace in those times when we *feel* unspiritual or dry or lacking in faith and zeal.

"Lord, I believe. Help my unbelief."

Our confidence must be *in the Lord*, not in the strength of our faith. When we place our confidence in our own faith level or zeal, we are essentially trusting in *ourselves*. But our trust cannot be in *our ability* to work up perfect faith or our ability to somehow *qualify* for receiving from God or serving Him. Our trust must be in the sufficiency of God Himself.

HIS STRENGTH PERFECTED IN MY WEAKNESS

> But He (the Lord) said to me, 'My grace is sufficient for you, for power is made perfect in weakness.' Therefore, I will boast all the more gladly in my weaknesses, so that the power of Messiah may dwell in me. For Messiah's sake, then, I delight in weaknesses...For when I am weak, then I am strong (2 Corinthians 12:9–10).

Paul identifies the recognizing of *weakness* as a starting point for receiving grace. Those whose trust is in their own ability will not see themselves as *needing* grace. No matter who we are, or how gifted or accomplished we might be, our greatest need is for the Lord Himself to reach into our humanity and pull us up into the place of His divine empowerment. The empowerment we need may be in areas where we have struggled, or areas of our walk where we want to further excel.

In either case, our victories and breakthroughs do not come from our striving to try to "work up" a faith that "qualifies" for the grace we need. We come into grace by *trusting* in the One who is totally sufficient. He is the One who is faithful to meet us amid our own lack or weakness. This is key to walking in God's *grace*.

Trusting in myself, in the strength of *my own* faith or spirituality, will just leave me discouraged. Why? Because I am aware that my own faith falls short. As much as I *desire* to be strong and faith-filled at all times, it is simply not the reality. But feeling my weakness does not have to leave me discouraged, as I learn to look to the Lord for what I lack. He is the One who *never changes*. If my confidence is in Him who never changes, and in the grace He imparts for my *becoming* more *like Him*, then my weaknesses do not have to be a limitation to my ultimate progress and growth.

Again, this is not to suggest that we should be *content* with the level where we are currently. Certainly we should not be *content* with unbelief. We cannot be satisfied with doubts and times when we feel down or defeated. Rather, in our own weakness, we look to God as the One who alone can lift us into the transforming work of grace. While perfect faith is a good and worthy goal, it is not a prerequisite for receiving all that we need for life, godliness, and fruitfulness. Our sufficiency comes from the Lord, not ourselves. *He* is the One who meets us in the place of our weakness. He makes up for all that we lack.

CORRIE TEN BOOM: A POWERFUL EXAMPLE OF LOOKING TO THE LORD

An account from the life of Corrie ten Boom provides us with a powerful example of walking out this principle. Corrie ten Boom helped Jews in Holland escape capture by the Nazis during the Holocaust of World War II. She and her family, motivated by their strong Christian faith, hid many Jewish people in their home. Eventually, the entire ten Boom family was arrested and sent to the concentration camps. Corrie, alone, survived the camp, while the rest of her family died there. After the war, Corrie ministered in many nations, typically sharing about the power of forgiveness and the love of God.

In a documentary about Corrie's life and legacy, the narrator described a time when Corrie was speaking at a church in Germany after the war. As she was speaking, she noticed a man in the audience who looked familiar. She suddenly realized who he was. He had been a German guard in the concentration camp where she and her sister, Betsie, had been imprisoned. This guard had been particularly cruel to Betsie, who had died in the camp. However, after the war ended, by God's grace, the guard had become a believer in Jesus. He, of course, remembered Corrie and Betsie well, and he felt compelled to approach Corrie after she spoke. He identified himself to her, explaining that he had prayed that God would give him the opportunity to ask forgiveness from one of his former victims. He extended his hand to her, asking her to forgive him, but Corrie stood stunned, *unable* to take his hand. Pamela Rosewell Moore, Corrie's traveling companion, describes this encounter:

> What happened next must have happened in seconds...Corrie stood there looking at him, and she knew she couldn't do it...All she could think of was Betsie's suffering. But then...she made a quick turning to (the Lord) and said, "Lord, help," and on that prayer, she received a verse into her heart and mind from Romans 5, "the love of God is brought into our hearts by the Holy Spirit who is given to us," and with that came a revelation: she was not expected to conjure, out of her own heart and mind, love for the man, but she could receive through the Holy Spirit that which was needed to forgive him...[2]

---

2 Robert Fernandez, Dir., *Corrie ten Boom: A Faith Undefeated* (Worcester, PA: Vision Video, 2013), DVD.

In those few moments, Corrie asked God to forgive her for the bitterness she felt, thanking Him for bringing His love to her heart through the Holy Spirit. Immediately, the Lord took away her bitterness, filling her with an overflowing sense of the freedom God's love brings to our hearts. She recalls thinking at that moment, "Thank You, Father, that Your love in me is victorious over my hatred. And at that moment my hatred disappeared."[3]

Notice what is described here. This great woman of God recognized, in a moment of need, that it simply *was not in* her to forgive the guard. But while recognizing her bitterness, she did not stop there, as if to hope that *maybe* one day she would be *able* to forgive the man.

> *This great woman of God recognized, in a moment of need, that it simply was not in her to forgive the guard.*

In the brief moments of the situation, it is important for us to note what Corrie *did* as well as what she did *not* do. She did *not* try to "fake" it or go through the motions of forgiving, while still feeling bitterness. She did not attempt to "work up" feelings of forgiveness. She knew she had to *resolve* her bitterness, yet she felt powerless to do so. She realized that what was required of her was literally a *supernatural* act, and what she needed for such an act was *grace*. What she needed was *supernatural* love and empowerment. She was unwilling to settle for just trying to make it through this encounter without dealing with the barriers in her own heart. She knew she had to interact with this man, and love was the only appropriate response. But she also saw that her own love was insufficient. Only God can provide such love. Thus, she looked to the Lord, the all-sufficient One. She looked to the One who *Himself is* perfect love so that she would be empowered to love and forgive the guard.

Notice, as well, that Corrie did not sink into condemnation and a sense of failure, thinking, "Oh, I cannot forgive the

---

3 Ibid.

man. I must be a terrible person." Too often, I suspect we can *stop* at the point of recognizing our human weakness, wrongly assuming we are stuck there and can go no further. We can then sink into condemnation, berating ourselves over why we are not more like Yeshua. However, Corrie looked to the Lord, who is the source of everything we need, and she was empowered to do the impossible. Grace enabled her to do what was unreasonable.

THE ONLY SOLUTION

The only answer to our natural shortcomings is seeing God's grace and *resting* in that grace, especially in those moments when our own weaknesses are so glaring to us. God delights in meeting us at the point of our weakness, but we must *look* to Him. He is not expecting us to *measure* up; rather, He wants us to *look* up. Can you see the difference? Trying to measure up will leave us trapped under the weight of our failures and condemnation. But *looking* up, as we recognize our weakness, positions us to receive grace and impartation from the Lord, taking us beyond our natural limitations and even our failures.

Seeing her need, Corrie's simple petition, "Lord, help," is much like the desperate prayer of the man noted earlier from Mark 9, as he cried to Yeshua: "Lord, I believe! Help my unbelief!" The same idea can be expressed in relation to so many aspects of our walk in which grace is required. Perhaps we are in a situation in which *courage* is needed, but we find ourselves more aware of the *fear* tugging at our hearts. Our prayer can be, "Lord, I choose courage, yet I feel the tug of fear on my heart. Help my lack of courage." Perhaps our need is for *perseverance* in some trial we are going through. "Lord, I choose perseverance, but I can feel the weariness and the desire to give up. Help me in my lack of endurance." Maybe our pressing need is for supernatural *love* and compassion. "Lord, I choose to be gracious and loving, but I feel the pull of self-centeredness. Help me in the hardness of my heart."

I could mention many more examples, but hopefully the point is clear. The *idea* of the simple prayer, "Lord, I believe.

Help my unbelief," can be expressed in many forms and different situations of need. In praying this way, we are expressing to God the "yes" in our hearts, even as we recognize the weakness in our flesh. In praying this way, we are not content to be stuck in our weakness, but we are looking to Him to be the all-sufficient One who wants to provide in every area where we lack. Trusting in His provision and sufficiency, we can then step out in faith, believing He will meet us with His enablement.

We are looking to His grace to take us beyond what we ourselves are capable of. Looking to His grace, we come into a freedom from *striving* to produce from our*selves* something we do not have. This is part of what it means to *rest* in the sufficiency of God.

THE BALANCE BETWEEN *RESTING* AND *REACHING*

There is an important balance we must keep in mind, as we consider the principle of *resting* in God's sufficiency. We must realize that *resting* is not the same as *inactivity*. We are *not inactive* in looking to God for our sufficiency. We simply are realizing that what we need for life and godliness is found *in Him*, not in ourselves. Seeing this, we come to terms with what can seem like conflicting principles. We *rest* in God and put our trust in Him rather than *striving* to attain to godliness in our own strength. At the same time, we are to "*press on* toward the goal for the reward of the upward calling of God in Messiah Yeshua" (Phil. 3:14, italics added).

These, too, are the words of Paul, who seemed to understand that our life in God calls for a balance between *constant pursuit* of growth in godliness, while looking to the Lord as the One who makes such growth possible. Paul grasped the balance between *resting* in God's sufficiency, yet continually *reaching higher* to experience more of that sufficiency. Reaching higher does not speak of striving. It speaks of *aiming* higher than our present experience. Thus, we can be continually reaching forward in our walk with God without feeling driven by a sense of failure and not measuring up. The key to this balance is the glorious *relationship* with God, made possible by His unreasonable grace. Confidence in our relationship with Him helps us experience true *rest*, as we continue to reach forward for more of what God has for our lives, even as we are aware of our weaknesses and failures.

Don't look to yourself to try to produce something you do not have. That is the essence of striving. Striving is essentially our *natural* response to weaknesses we can see in ourselves. God's provision of *grace* is far superior to our striving. We must be alert to the tendencies we can have in this regard. *My efforts* to be righteous or holy or spiritual will never be the key to my victory. The key is found in my *trusting* what Yeshua has done *for* me, looking to Him daily for what I don't have, and stepping out in faith as I trust in His provision.

CONCLUDING THOUGHTS

When we embrace Yeshua as Messiah, Savior, and Lord, we enter a glorious journey overseen by God Himself. God's desire and plan is to be totally *involved* in our lives. You and I are works in progress, and the Lord fully intends to continue and complete the good work He has begun in us (see Philippians 1:6).

What is that good work? He is bringing about an ongoing transformation, resulting in our *becoming* more like Yeshua Himself. This is our destiny! As we are becoming like Yeshua, we also have the privilege of bearing His name, representing Him to an unbelieving world that desperately needs a revelation of who God is. God's plan is that you and I, in the uniqueness of our individual callings and assignments, are to *be* that revelation. Such a goal would be utterly unreasonable, except for the fact that God imparts *grace* to us for what would otherwise be impossible. God's grace connects us to a life that is *beyond reason*. Our part is to daily enter by faith *into* this grace.

There is certainly much more that could be said about grace. While covering much ground, this book really just represents an introduction to this vast subject. Each day, we will likely encounter different opportunities and decisions, either to enter the realm of God's grace or to live out our lives in the confines of our natural limitations. God has an *overflow* of grace prepared for you and me. He intends for us to live victoriously, and He wants to give us the grace that makes victory a reality.

Remember, the realm of God's grace is a realm in which there are no impossibilities. Because of His grace, we can be a forward-looking people of faith, hope, and expectation. We are people of *His Kingdom*. Our destiny is to walk in righteousness, peace, and joy in the Holy Spirit, as we live to be a blessing to the world around us. What makes this possible is a grace that is beyond reason.

The question for us is simply, are we willing to *receive* the overflow of grace that we need and then live our lives believing His grace is at work in us? It is His amazing gift to us. We cannot earn it, and we will never deserve it, yet grace is there for us to fully receive as a gift from God. This is our inheritance! This is the promise of God that is key to lifting our lives into a realm of supernatural empowerment and victory, in spite of ourselves.

Don't try to figure out grace. Don't try to fully understand it or make sense of it. Remember, grace is unreasonable. Ask God daily to help you walk in that childlike faith that learns to simply *receive* with a grateful heart. Ask Him daily for fresh revelation of this grace, even as Paul prayed for the believers in Ephesus:

> (God) may give to you the spirit of *wisdom and revelation* in the knowledge of Him, the *eyes of your understanding being enlightened*; that you may know what is the *hope of His calling*, what are the *riches of the glory of His inheritance* in the saints, and what is the exceeding greatness of His power toward us who believe, according to the working of His mighty power... (Ephesians 1:17–19, NKJV, italics added).

May this be our *prayer*, and may this be our growing *experience* all the days of our lives!

ABOUT THE AUTHOR

Jerry Miller is a Messianic Jew who came to faith in Yeshua (Jesus) in 1975. Jerry and his wife Jo have served the Lord in ministry for almost forty years in the Messianic movement and beyond. Their ministry has been multi-faceted, as they have served in teaching, personal mentoring, worship leading, biblical counseling, and numerous projects related to unity among Jewish and Gentile believers in Yeshua. For almost thirty years Jerry and Jo were in pastoral ministry, leading Messianic congregations in Maryland and Florida. In 2013 they launched into a new season of ministry focus, involving travel throughout the USA and internationally, teaching in congregations, Bible schools and other settings. Central to this new season has been their passion for raising up the younger generations, seeing them equipped, discipled and embracing their destinies for serving God's Kingdom purposes. Much of Jerry and Jo's current focus involves travel to Messianic congregations, where they work with congregational leaders and leadership teams. They also minister in churches building bridges of unity, desiring to help fulfill the biblical mandate of One New Man in Messiah (Eph. 2:15). Jerry and Jo have been married for more than 44 years and have two daughters and five grandchildren.

Visit their website for more information at www.GraceEmpowers.org.

If you are interested in inviting Jerry and Jo to minister at your congregation or conference, send an email to jerrymil77@gmail.com.

IF YOU'RE A FAN OF THIS BOOK, WILL YOU HELP ME SPREAD THE WORD?

THERE ARE SEVERAL WAYS YOU CAN HELP ME GET THE WORD OUT ABOUT THE MESSAGE OF THIS BOOK...

- Post a 5-Star review on Amazon.
- Write about the book on your Facebook, Twitter, Instagram, LinkedIn – any social media you regularly use!
- If you blog, consider referencing the book, or publishing an excerpt from the book with a link back to my website. You have my permission to do this as long as you provide proper credit and backlinks.
- Recommend the book to friends – word-of-mouth is still the most effective form of advertising.
- Purchase additional copies to give away as gifts.
- Purchase a copy for your pastor or Messianic rabbi.

The best way to connect is by visiting www.GraceEmpowers.org.